A CATHOLIC GUIDE to $PENDING LESS and Living More

"Do you want to retire early, but you're not sure how to do it while raising a family? Learn from a couple who are not only doing it, they're doing it on one income *and* they have fourteen kids!"

Brandon Ganch
"The Mad Fientist"
Financial expert and host of *Financial Independence Podcast*

"This guide is a timely antidote to the materialistic fallacy that more stuff means more happiness."

From the foreword by **Gary Zimak**
Author of *Give Up Worry for Lent!* and *Let Go of Anger and Stress!*

"With their on-fire faith, extra-large family, and big dreams, Sam and Rob Fatzinger are sure to inspire you. No more excuses! This gem of a book is filled with good faith, humor, and practical advice to help you get your financial house in order."

Danielle Bean
Author, speaker, and brand manager of CatholicMom.com

"*A Catholic Guide to Spending Less and Living More* draws solidly from scripture and springs from the authors' interesting family experience. The Fatzingers speak with wisdom and the authority that results from combining two of the most important criteria for addressing any topic: scripture and personal experience. Their wisdom and counsel can help anyone manage their money successfully and with deeper faith."

Fr. Michael White and Tom Corcoran
Authors of *ChurchMoney* and *Rebuilt*

"If Rob and Sam Fatzinger can live a debt-free life with fourteen kids, so can you! It takes commitment, prayer, attention to detail, and a good sense of humor to make it all work. Their guide is a must-read for anyone interested in simplifying their life, becoming financially stable, and living their Catholic faith."

Jon and Evelyn Bean
Cofounders of Compass Catholic Ministries

ADVICE FROM A DEBT-FREE FAMILY OF 16

A CATHOLIC GUIDE
to
$PENDING LESS
and
Living More

Sam and Rob Fatzinger

Ave Maria Press   AVE   Notre Dame, Indiana

Foreword © 2021 by Gary Zimak

Founded in 1865, Ave Maria Press is a ministry of the United States Province of Holy Cross.

www.avemariapress.com

Paperback: ISBN-13 978-1-64680-047-6

E-book: ISBN-13 978-1-64680-048-3

Cover image © gettyimages.com

Cover design by Katherine Robinson.

Text design by Sam Watson.

Printed and bound in the United States of America.

Library of Congress Cataloging-in-Publication Data
Names: Fatzinger, Sam, author. | Fatzinger, Rob, author.
Title: A Catholic guide to spending less and living more : advice from a debt-free family of 16 / Sam and Rob Fatzinger.
Description: Notre Dame, Indiana : Ave Maria Press, 2021. | Includes bibliographical references and index. | Summary: "In this book, the parents of fourteen children share their story of living on a modest income and show how Catholic values and mindsets can lead to a life of financial freedom"-- Provided by publisher.
Identifiers: LCCN 2020045230 | ISBN 9781646800476 (paperback) | ISBN 9781646800483 (ebook)
Subjects: LCSH: Finance, Personal--Religious aspects--Catholic Church. | Quality of life--Religious aspects--Catholic Church.
Classification: LCC HG179 .F37 2021 | DDC 332.0240088/282--dc23
LC record available at https://lccn.loc.gov/2020045230

TO OUR FAMILY AND FRIENDS.

YOU WERE INSTRUMENTAL

IN OUR JOURNEY OF BLESSINGS.

WITHOUT YOUR INSPIRATION AND INFLUENCE,

THIS BOOK WOULD NOT HAVE BEEN POSSIBLE.

CONTENTS

FOREWORD

Count your blessings.

Once upon a time, not so long ago, this expression captured a way of life that truly allowed people to, as the title of this book suggests, "spend less and live more." Unfortunately this message has gotten lost as a new cultural principle has emerged: more stuff means more happiness.

The book you hold in your hands provides a timely antidote to this materialistic fallacy. In *A Catholic Guide to Spending Less and Living More,* Rob and Sam Fatzinger remind us of the riches of spiritual poverty, a message preached and lived by Jesus. For more than thirty years, the Fatzingers have taken this message to heart—, and in this book, they affirm that living simply is what brings happiness. It's a message that we all need to hear!

For as long as I can remember, I have always enjoyed having stuff. Starting in early childhood and continuing right through my forties, I collected baseball cards, comic books, records, videos, memorabilia, and many other items. But despite having all these items in my possession, I rarely took the time to enjoy them. I was never satisfied, and I kept acquiring more and more, having bought into the myth that more possessions meant more happiness.

When I was thirty-five, I met and married my wife, Eileen, and we settled into a condo and lived a comfortable life. Eileen had a modest upbringing and wasn't used to spending money, but I began to teach her all about the "joy" of eating out and buying things we didn't really need. After a few years, we purchased a home in anticipation of starting a family. When our twins, Mary and Elizabeth, were born three years later, our spending habits remained more or less the same. Then we decided that Eileen would quit her job to be a stay-at-home mom. While this was a great decision, we—no, I—never stopped to consider the effect that a new house, two additional family members and one less income would have. Soon we were buried in $20,000 of credit card debt.

As the girls grew older and the years passed, we managed to make some short-term changes and pay off our debt (courtesy of a home equity loan), but it didn't last. I worked hard, and made a decent wage as a software developer. But I still enjoyed spending money and was still into collecting things (mainly DVDs, CDs, and books at this point). We all enjoyed fast food and other treats. After all, who doesn't need a "pick me up" every now and then? My non existent financial planning skills and careless spending were once again leading us down a dangerous path. Before long, our credit card balance was right back where it was before. Another home equity loan solved the problem, at least for a while.

Several years later, a medical scare caused my faith to flourish, and I began to follow Jesus in a more serious way. Then, in 2012, I was laid off from my job as a software developer. With Eileen's encouragement, I seized the opportunity to begin a career as a full-time Catholic speaker and author. Once again, I never took the time to consider the financial challenges that we would face. Preoccupied with homeschooling our daughters and caring for the needs of our family, Eileen continued let me "handle" the finances. Once again, I came up short. Not only were we soon buried in $25,000 of credit card debt but also we owed $8,000 in income tax. Something had to be done.

Eileen and I made the difficult decision to sell our single home and move into a mobile home. The four of us moved into a 1,100 square foot, two-bedroom living space. It was a painful process that required selling or donating most of our furniture and possessions. In addition, all of my toys (books, collectibles, and assorted memorabilia) ended up being sold at yard sales. My new office became the dining room table, and I relied on headphones to block out distractions. All of us struggled greatly during the transition period.

Now, here's the good news: This hard, humiliating lesson finally taught us to live within our means! We have been debt free for two years. By choosing to live modestly, our family has grown closer to the Lord and closer to each other. After mindlessly praying the words "give us this day our daily bread" for decades, I now understand what it means to depend on the Father's providence. We're in a good place now, but we had to go through some very rough days to get here. Rather than simply tell you that everything worked out fine for us, my desire is to help you to avoid the pain caused by the pursuit of material pleasure.

God really does care how we spend our money. This is the important message you will discover in the pages that follow, as Rob and Sam Fatzinger share the story of how they achieved financial freedom— and show how you can, too. Following their advice will not only free you from the unnecessary burden of debt and the endless pursuit of "more" but it will also draw you closer to God.

What you are about to read is not some pie-in-the-sky collection of fluff but a practical and effective instruction manual for living the Gospel, written by people who practice what they preach. I'm honored that I was asked to write a few words and present to you a way of living that will change your life for the better. As you prepare to turn the page and begin your journey, I urge you to keep an open mind. The message delivered by the Fatzingers will often seem at odds with the "wisdom" of the world. That's not a bad thing. Their ideas and lifestyle mirror the plan laid out by Jesus, whose message was also considered by many to be countercultural. In the end, following him is what matters most.

Gary Zimak
Bestselling author, speaker, and radio host

INTRODUCTION

(Sam)

On a warm spring day in 1988, my boyfriend, Rob (age twenty-four), and I (age twenty) were sitting on top of Sugarloaf Mountain in Maryland enjoying a picnic lunch when Rob blurted out, "Will you marry me?"

I replied, "Of course I will marry you, someday."

Rob said, "No, I mean, let's get married soon, for real. I'm asking you to marry me." After I gave him a skeptical look, he said, "Who else is gonna give you ten kids, a dog, and a house with a white picket fence?" There may have also been something mentioned about being tossed off the mountain if the answer was no.

"Forget the dog," I countered. "Make it eleven kids and the answer is yes!" We were married one year later, got pregnant on our honeymoon, and began our journey.

But our journey to financial freedom really started when we were children; our upbringing instilled in us financial habits that influence us both to this day. The path to financial freedom has no end. We are still traveling it—sometimes for better and sometimes for worse, but never in boredom—and we would like to encourage you in your own efforts toward financial security and peace.

Rob and I have been married for more than thirty years. You may be wondering about my nickname, Sam; I got it fifty-some years ago from my four older brothers, whom I adore. My given name is Cecilia, but when they started calling me "Sam," it stuck like glue!

Rob and I have fourteen kids and seven grandchildren. We have lived in the same town for more than fifty years. Rob has been the primary breadwinner, and I have had the harder and more rewarding job of being a stay-at-home mom. We are a regular *Leave It to Beaver* family, minus the pearls and well-behaved kids. Our oldest eight kids are out of the house now, in college or working. Throughout this book, you will find suggestions, advice, helpful hints, and words of encouragement from our older kids. We are delighted to see that our children are living out the habits of good stewardship and financial security that helped Rob and me. We hope you will find this inspiring, too!

Can you really spend less and live more, as the title of this book suggests? For more than thirty years, we have been living that particular dream, and we are eager to share our path to financial freedom with you. As you will discover from our story, you don't have to be a Warren Buffett and have a net worth measured in the billions to live well— or to be financially secure. That comes from a combination of

- spending less than you make,
- saving for emergencies and eventualities,
- being generous with your resources,
- living debt-free,
- learning to be intentional spenders and careful consumers, and
- giving yourself the option to retire early.

Basically, it is about embracing good stewardship—and the virtues associated with recognizing God as the source of all we have—in a way that provides financial flexibility so that you control the money, rather than allowing it to control you. It is about setting and achieving financial goals (and continually revising and expanding those goals) to accomplish all you believe God is calling you to do.

It hasn't been all rainbows and unicorns. Any goal, be it financial or otherwise, requires self-discipline and commitment, and involves making choices (sometimes hard choices) about how to get the life you want to have. You must really want to save money. You must really want to pay down debt. You must really want to do the will of God! Really? Yes, really.

It can be hard to control your budget and spending. If you don't have a solid plan of action, you will just keep falling back into the same old bad financial habits. We know, because we have made all kinds of financial mistakes and tried to learn from them. Hopefully, learning about our setbacks and experiences can help you avoid some of the same financial pitfalls.

A Word to Couples

If you are married, husbands and wives really must be on the same page, or this adventure toward financial independence will be rough on you both. In the Catholic Church, marriage is a sacrament, and the graces of that sacrament give us the strength to parent well. We must unite as a couple and support each other, especially when financial struggles appear. One of my favorite sayings, from Mike and Alicia Hernon, the founders of the *Messy Family Project*, is, "It's better to be wrong together than right alone!"[1]

My husband and I are a team. We help each other, according to our strengths and weaknesses, with all things financial. For thirty-something years, we have shared a dream of living debt-free and retiring early, all while being true to our faith—and for the most part, we have stayed on track. But when we did derail our finances, we picked ourselves up and resumed the journey. Now we feel that it is our turn to help others with the struggle to live a simpler, financially mindful lifestyle. Rob always tells people, "I'm good with money, and Sam doesn't like to spend it!" Of course, it helped when we didn't have any money to spend in those early years.

So, how about you? What financial issues keep you awake at night or create conflict between the two of you? What are the sneaky little habits (or the big, hard-to-break ones) that keep you living paycheck to paycheck? Do you need financial wisdom or more self-control (or maybe both) to help you find financial freedom, contentment, a stronger faith, and peace in this buy-more, live-bigger world in which we live? You may think it is impossible in today's world to "make it" financially. The truth is, it can be very challenging at times—but with God's help it's not impossible.

Spending Less and Living More Is for Everyone

Don't let that last bit addressed to couples scare you off if you are making this journey to financial security on your own. While the specifics of your challenges will be different from ours, many of the principles about saving and spending are the same. (And frankly, it can be easier to track your spending when just one person is holding the checkbook.)

Maybe you're a single adult or a college student determined not to be saddled with piles of student debt upon graduation. Good for you! Maybe you've made some unfortunate choices or life has slammed you hard, and you are trying to dig your way out. Stick with us; I promise this book has something for you, too.

Some people start seeking financial stability once the absence of it becomes a roadblock to realizing their dreams. It may be that debt is hindering thoughts of a call to the priesthood or religious life or preventing you from being open to adding another child to an already tight budget. Or maybe you are done raising your family and just want to enjoy life after all those hard years of sacrificing financially for the kids but are unable to do so because the economy ate up your investments. We hear you, and we feel your pain!

Whatever your situation, our family has been (and in some cases, still is) where you are. We have older kids that we still worry about and younger ones at home, down to the age of four. Our careful plans have been shaken up by events beyond our control (like the 2020 coronavirus pandemic), and it will take some time to get things back on track. But we have already started picking up the pieces. And so, my friend, can you.

So, pull up a chair, put up your feet, grab your sacrifice beads and your favorite beverage (adult or otherwise), and spend a few hours with us. We'd like to share our story with you and offer concrete advice to help you achieve your own financial goals, conquer your challenges, and strengthen your faith.

About This Book

This book is divided into two parts. The first part includes six "big ideas" based on Christian principles of good stewardship—virtues that God has been cultivating in our family that have helped us overcome enslavement to stuff, choose contentment, seek his plan, live generously, spend intentionally, and embrace community. The second part of the book is Rob's brainchild: It gives you specific habits and skills to identify, execute, and achieve your particular financial goals—the things that will help *you* live more and spend less. These skills include living debt-free (perhaps on one modest income, as we have done for most of our lives), planning for retirement, easing money-related anxieties, and teaching kids to be good money managers, faithful stewards, and discerning consumers.

We hope that as you read this book you will have in your sights the most important achievement of all: Knowing what it means to trust and follow God and his plan for your life. For many of us, that entails a strong marriage and happy family life. For all of us, it entails being a good steward of your God-given resources and talents.

At the end of most chapters we've included questions to help you in the discernment process. You can use a little notebook (write "SLAM" or "Spend Less, Achieve More" on the cover, so you are constantly reminded of the reason for doing all this hard work!) to jot down notes and ideas that strike you as you move through the chapters, or even write in the margins of the book or use a highlighter to mark the personally relevant parts.

If you need special help paying for college, getting your food budget under control, planning a wedding, or creating a customized family budget, we have created specific downloadable resources for those. Check them out on the Ave Maria Press website at www.avemariapress.com/products/catholic-guide-to-spending-less-and-living-more or our website at FatzFam.

com. Feel free to drop us a note with any questions or helpful money-saving ideas you've discovered along the way—maybe one day we'll write another book!

+JMJ+

PART 1

SIX BIG IDEAS FOR FINANCIAL FREEDOM: MINDSETS MATTER

(Sam)

One day my friend and her husband stopped by, and the husband looked out into our backyard and said, "Oh, bummer. Your dryer broke."

I had no idea what he was talking about. "No, why do you say that?" He pointed out back to my two clotheslines packed full of clothes. "Ah," I said, "I just hang clothes out on the line when it's sunny." Using a clothesline not only saves money on our utility bill but it gets stains out of clothes like no other cleaner.

Maybe you already hang your clothes on the line because you prefer the smell of fresh air to dryer sheets, and you haven't thought about the saving-money angle. That's good! This book isn't just about how to save money—it's also about how to enhance the quality of your life. Especially in this first part, we're going to talk about attitudes and virtues that, taken all together, will help you live better and spend less—that is, to be more intentional about how you use the resources God has given you.

Thousands of articles and books are available that have tips for saving money—as a Catholic family of sixteen, we've read a lot of them! At the end of this book we've included a list of resources that we have found most helpful in case you need advice in a specific area. But in this book we want to share things that have worked for us to achieve financial freedom and live debt-free. We hope that these practical money-saving tips and solutions will encourage you to live better and spend less, too. And it all starts with making small changes in the way we live and think. Saving those nickels and dimes—and making money-saving habits—quickly becomes second nature when you put your mind to it!

So what are these "big ideas," these mindsets that have helped us to become better stewards of the things God has given us?

- Take stock and dream big (create a "financial vision" and execute the plan).
- Be a good steward for life.
- Become an intentional spender.
- Practice contentment.
- Be generous.
- Choose to trust.

As you look over these ideas, do any of them jump out at you as an area of opportunity for growth? Have you ever stopped to consider that it might hold the key not just to financial freedom but also to your family's long-term happiness?

Are you happy with your financial state? If you are reading this book, you are looking for something. Maybe you are trying to plan for your future in a time of uncertainty, or you hope to make a special purchase—a new car, a great vacation, or a house. Or maybe you are looking at your bank and credit card statements with a sinking heart and wishing there was a way to get back on track. No matter what it is that caused you to choose this book from the hundreds available, we want to encourage you to let God show you how pursuing *your* financial vision can be an opportunity for spiritual growth, just as it has been for us.

Of course, one little book is no substitute for sound personal advice from someone who knows you and your situation. You should get the help you need from a trusted mentor or financial advisor to fine-tune your plan based on what you read here and what works best for your family. But it is also essential that you find time for prayer, asking God to inspire you to create a plan that pleases him and puts you and your family on the path to financial freedom.

> For I know well the plans that I have in mind for you—oracle of the LORD—plans for your welfare and not for woe, so as to give you a future of hope.
> —Jeremiah 29:11

ONE

TAKE STOCK AND DREAM BIG
(Sam)

From the age of ten until I was twelve, I had a paper route. It was a weekly local paper that I delivered every Thursday. I only was paid 10 cents per paper. Each month I would get a $26 paycheck. It doesn't seem like much now, but at ten years old I felt a sense of pride from that paycheck. I hated the idea of blowing money that I worked hard for on a toy or a snack that would be gone in a moment. Whenever I got a paycheck or earned some cash from mowing lawns or shoveling snow, I would put nearly all of it in my bank account. By the age of fourteen, I had saved more than $3,000. Even though I didn't realize it at the time, this would pay for my first car, my cell phone bill, and even part of my community college.
—**Joey Fatzinger**, age twenty-three

Let's say you're driving home from an early appointment and have a few spare minutes. You know you have a long day ahead of you—cleaning, cooking, work notes to go over—and then you see the Starbucks sign ahead.

13

I totally deserve a special drink you think. *I have a busy day ahead, and I could really use the caffeine shot!* Then you remember the discussion you had with your spouse about the recent credit card payments and the bills that are past due, and you realize that every dollar counts. Not to mention, how would you explain it when your spouse cleans out the car and finds your old cup in the drink holder? You decide to pass Starbucks and ask God to use this small sacrifice to bless your marriage and give you wisdom about better ways to save money.

Congratulations! You have just made a commitment toward your financial freedom.

Even if you don't have (or think you need) a structured financial plan, making that choice to skip the macchiato and make an iced coffee at home brings you one step closer to creating the life you want with the resources you have. And it all begins with your mind, or (more precisely) your financial mindset.

We want to work with you to create and implement a *financial vision* for your life—a kind of "master financial plan." Once we established our own vision (step 1), we set specific goals that would allow us to live this vision (step 2), identified obstacles to achieving those goals (step 3), and created a plan to overcome those obstacles (step 4). For the rest of this chapter, we will share more about these four important steps in order to help you create your own financial plan. So, grab your SLAM (Spend Less, Achieve More) notebook and pen, and take some notes. Let's take a look at four key questions.

Step 1: What Is Your Financial Vision?

When Rob and I got married, we shared a big financial vision. It had three parts: We wanted to serve God and the Church, raise a big family, and use our assets, talents, and time in a way that pleases God. You could say that was our first financial vision, although at the time we didn't write it down or speak of it exactly in those terms. I just constantly prayed, and still do, "Thy will be done! Dear Lord, grant me wisdom, prudence, and self-control. And please give these virtues to my family, too."

Looking at the big picture from the outset helped us achieve specific goals we set along the way. For example, I found it easier not to spend money when I knew Rob was putting away money to buy our dream home. When we finally heard of a foreclosure on the potential dream house with a big yard in the neighborhood wanted to live in, I got excited. And when I knew we had saved enough to afford the down payment; I breathed a sigh of relief. Now we could slow down our rate of savings, right?

Well, we did relax our budget some after we bought the house and closed our business (more about our bookstore later). We could spend a bit more each month because Rob's new job supplied a regular paycheck, paid time off, and health insurance. But Rob also found a new goal: he wanted to pay off the house early, starting with the very first mortgage payment. And because we had already learned to stay within a certain budget, there wasn't a big difference in our daily spending habits when he started adding extra money to every mortgage payment. Life just went on as usual, except I bought paper towels occasionally.

That big, beautiful house was an important goal for us, but we kept on saving because it was only part of the financial vision we had established that would chart the course of our life together. This was our vision in a nutshell: Don't spend money unless necessary so we can afford to be open to life and stay home with our kids.

What is *your* financial vision? Think about it, talk about it with your spouse, and write it in your notebook.

Step 2: What Are Your Financial Goals?

Unlike your financial vision, which establishes the trajectory of
your life, your financial goals are the milestone markers, important steps to achieving that vision. Some will likely require long-
term financial planning, but others might cost little or no money
at all. Here's what one daughter had to say:

> Have goals and an idea of how you want your life to
> look but be flexible because things will not always
> (basically never) turn out the way you plan. Make
> smart decisions now, the kind that will support the
> kind of future you want: Start investing. Choose a
> good college that will not put you in a ton of debt.
> Hang around good people that build you up. (Lizzie
> Fatzinger Rowedder, age twenty-six)

We started setting our financial goals before we were even
married, sitting there on the top of Sugarloaf Mountain. We
worked at it during the course of that year, so that by the time
our wedding day arrived, we had already laid the groundwork
for how we were going to live as a married couple.

We began by setting a budget so we could see that we were
spending less than we made—even while planning our wedding—and made sure that we continued to tithe to our church
and give to other charities (in time and money). We surrounded
ourselves with good role models and mentors, and we trusted
that God would take care of us, no matter what.

We planned a simple wedding and took the money Rob's dad
offered us for our wedding to put a down payment on a town
house. We chose the least expensive town house we could find
in the nicest neighborhood. Once we had paid off the balance
on the small amount of debt Rob had accrued during school,

we began saving my salary from working part-time at a daycare center. We knew we wanted to live on Rob's salary so that I could stay home with any kids God might choose to send us, so we figured we should start living that way right from the start.

As our family has grown over the years, we have all set goals to help us get the life we want. The kids worked to set up car and college funds. We set up emergency and retirement funds. We scheduled a time for daily prayer, individually and as a family. We made a choice to homeschool our kids (except for one, whom we found a great program that meets his needs much better than we could).

What are some specific goals you have financially, short-term and long-term? Write them all down in your notebook—from the easiest, smallest ones to the largest, most outrageous ones. They are your goals, and only you and your spouse can decide if they have merit.

Let's look at three examples of common goals. (For information about achieving these goals, you can peek ahead at chapter 9, which covers saving.)

Set up an emergency fund.

You hear it all the time from financial experts: "Set aside three months of expenses." "Have six months of expenses in a savings account for emergencies." We happen to agree with this, but how do you go about accomplishing this goal?

An emergency fund is a liquid savings account (not in the stock market or vintage Pokémon cards) containing enough money to live on (to pay basic expenses such as rent/mortgage, utilities, and food) in the case of life's unexpected events—losing your job, needing a new furnace or large car repair, or facing an unexpected medical expense. It's not for going out with the guys to the big game or getting the latest handbag that the Kardashians are pushing.

Retire by age sixty.

Saving for retirement . . . we all know we should be doing it. But there are many other things demanding our limited financial assets. Some of them are needs (food, housing, clothing), while some of them are wants (new shoes, the daily latte, a trip to the Bahamas).

Some people believe they should spend now and trust that God will take care of them when the time comes, like he's some kind of magical piggy bank. But is that really being a good steward? We believe that trusting God is definitely the key to all of this. I could talk for hours about all the times we had to rub two pennies together to make things work. Honestly, God did come through every time. And yet, like any good parent, he still expects us to do our part.

For now, I will persuade you in two little words why you should start saving early when it comes to a retirement fund: compound interest. Actually, they are two little words Rob taught me along with this story about two crazy kids called Jack and Diane. Jack and Diane both know they should save for retirement. And both have the same goal of saving a million dollars by the age of sixty-five. Both make investments that earn an annual return of 6 percent. And they both decide they will save $10,000 a year.

Jack spent the early years of his career buying BMWs and going to the Bahamas twice a year. He didn't start saving until age thirty-five but then saved $10,000 annually for the next thirty years until he was sixty-five. His results: He saved a total of $300,000 over those thirty years, and he now has an account balance of $838,019. Not too shabby!

Diane, however, was given a copy of this book as a gift when she finished grad school. She started saving at age twenty-five and continued putting aside $10,000 annually for the next fifteen years. When she turned forty, she stopped saving for retirement. Her results: That $150,000 saved over those fifteen years grew to $1,058,912 by the time she reached age sixty-five. She made even more money from half the investment, just by starting ten years sooner.

Compound interest is your friend. Don't wait to get started!

Give more.

_____

As you work to do what it takes to get on good financial footing, don't forget to pray for wisdom on how you can be of better service to other people (and of course to God). Even if you don't have debt, you may want to consider ways you can cut back in order to do more with your money to help God's people—to use your finances to be the hands and feet of our Savior.

Many people in our world need help, so narrow it down to something that speaks to your heart. If you have a relative struggling with Alzheimer's, look for groups that specialize in researching a cure. We found a group that works to free people from human trafficking when I was convicted to help in this area after watching the movie *Taken*.

If you are unsure about the best way to give, ask God to guide you to the right opportunities. Finances are very stressful and cause problems for couples, families, and single people; don't let your good intentions disturb your peace. One of Satan's most powerful tools is getting us to think that it is our money, not God's.

Now it's your turn: What are some goals that are important to you right now? Think about it, talk about your goals with your spouse, and write them down in your notebook.

Step 3: What's Holding You Back?

Being good stewards with our resources can be hard at times. Rob and I are so proud of the way our children have followed our example in living well while spending less. And yet, as our twenty-five-year-old daughter Barbara points out, it can be difficult to resist the temptation to spend:

> Self-control. So simple, so difficult, so not fun. This is something I have always struggled with. After all, I feel entitled to "treat myself" because I work so hard. I'm not in debt, I've never been in debt, and I save about 20 percent of my income. But I always go over budget. Like always. I over shop . . . a lot. By *a lot*, I just mean an unnecessary amount. My fun money budget is $200 a month, and I typically blow through that by the third week of the month. Impulse purchases are the bane of my existence (that and online shopping).

At some time or another, we all hit the wall, financially speaking. The unexpected happens and derails our carefully laid plans. Sometimes it is a mess of our own making (an overdrawn bank account, a totaled car, an ill-advised pair of Jimmy Choos), but sometimes life just happens (a medical catastrophe, natural disaster, or other "act of God").

Several years ago, our entire family flew to Arizona for the wedding of one of our children—a once-in-a-lifetime trip that made Rob swear off going to any wedding more than sixty minutes away. Just as our savings had recovered from the long-distance wedding expense, we had some medical issues that would have put us in a financial crisis if my husband hadn't been so diligent about building that fund back up. We call it the $40,000 tick bite: We paid more than $7,000, and insurance covered the rest. Our eight-year-old woke up one morning limping, and after a year of visits to two of the best hospitals in the DC, Maryland, and Virginia area, he was finally diagnosed with Lyme disease, now advanced. He had major hip surgery to reinsert his hip socket, and then a second surgery to remove the metal hardware so the TSA doesn't body-slam him every time he flies. Thanks be to God, he is doing great three years later, with no side effects.

These kinds of life happenings—whether one big one or dozens of smaller ones compounded over the years—can put *anybody's* bank account in a frenzy (even old penny-pinchers like us). There are always going to be unexpected situations to hurt your wallet. Some days we just roll our eyes, because the minute we pay off the new washer, the car dies. What's going on? Oh yeah, life.

The first step to getting back on track is to define the obstacles in your path. That means listing your financial problems. Do you and your spouse see eye to eye financially? Are you past due on loans or other bills? Did you have a recent job loss? Do you have an elderly parent in need of immediate help? Are you trying to pay for a wedding on a shoestring and running out of lace? Are you (like our daughter Barbara) running out of money before you run out of the month?

What are the current obstacles you are facing? Write them down in your notebook.

Step 4: What Are Possible Solutions?

Many high schools and colleges offer classes on problem-solving and life skills. These are skills we have taught the kids ourselves over the years (and that the older ones have taught to the younger ones) to help them get out of tricky situations without Mom and Dad figuring it out for them. Daily I say, "Figure it out yourself; this is a life skill. If you truly cannot figure it out, then I will help you." Too many college graduates still depend on Mom and Dad to get them out of trouble or to hand them the answers to life's common struggles.

No matter whether you are just starting out or have been running a household for years, an important part of "adulting" is recovering (and learning) from mistakes. And if you are a parent, one of the most powerful ways you can encourage your children toward adulthood is by letting them see you own your own messes. Let them see you and your spouse work together to identify problems, come up with solutions, and even ask for help, when needed.

So, what are your most pressing problems? One of the most common is Barbara's, in Step 3 too much month and too little paycheck. Who hasn't burned through their paycheck(s) before the end of the month arrives? I know we have, many a time. It was always a blessing when God pulled through for us, but we had to give him something to work with, and that is not spending unnecessarily. We lived paycheck-to-paycheck for about fifteen years. This isn't to say we never had enough. It is more like saying that God watched over and blessed us because we trusted *him* with our family and our future.

Even so, running out of money before the month's end is frustrating and stressful, and it can have humiliating and costly results, such as a bounced check and the accompanying fees. There is a simple, but not necessarily easy, solution to this recurring problem. Spend less than you make.

Simple, eh? Easy? Nah.

Some months, you just aren't going to have enough money. Life happens. For ten years we owned a Christian bookstore and only made money in December and the spring months. We learned to stash away savings in the busy months to get us through when sales were slow. These were savings from a regular account, not our emergency fund—that was for emergencies only.

So, you are thinking, *Okay, then what do we do if we can't use our emergency fund?*

First of all, the emergency fund is yours, so you *can* use it. That is better than having your power turned off or resorting to eating meatless Hamburger Helper. But your long-term financial recovery plan needs to include a budget and a savings account to tide you over during lean times. (More about that in chapter 7.)

What if you just don't have enough money coming in? We've been there, and it's not fun. In the past when we've had to beef up the savings or just needed to make a little more money to put food on the table, we've worked side jobs (mowing yards, childcare), had yard sales, and sold items on eBay. There was a time we were selling so many things that were just lying around the house, the kids were getting worried that they might be next. Seriously, though, if you really need immediate solutions about how to get ahead of the problem, you might want to sneak a peek at chapter 8.

So far, you've sketched out your financial vision and identified some of your goals as well as some of the most pressing obstacles. Now how are you coming along on the solutions? If you feel stuck, don't worry—this is just the first chapter, after all. Here are some ideas to get you started in figuring out solutions to the pressing problems that are holding you back from achieving your goals:

- If you are married, are you and your spouse having trouble getting on the same page? If so, find a financial planner, clergy member, or mentor that can help the two of you work toward a unified approach. Spend time before the Blessed Sacrament, asking God to give you wisdom and the humility to listen to each other and work together for the good of your whole family. You might also consider taking a financial course, such as Dave Ramsey's Financial Peace University.
- Too many bills? Make a list of all your debts and prioritize what to pay first as you think about some ways to raise extra cash.
- Recent job loss? Identify temporary stopgap measures while you work on decreasing expenses. Our son, who lost his job during the coronavirus lockdown, started delivering food for DoorDash.
- Having trouble trusting God? Take a leap of faith by doing something generous for someone else. It might surprise you how God comes through for those who earnestly seek to put others first. In the words of our daughter Lizzie: "I tried to be more intentional about tithing after I turned eighteen. Give first, save second, spend third."

Okay, now it's your turn. What are some possible solutions to the problems you are facing? If you can't think of anything, don't worry . . . just keep reading, and ask God to help you find the answers!

Don't Be Afraid!

This may all sound intimidating at first, but with God's help and some sacrifice and discipline, you can feel the freedom of overcoming debt and becoming financially secure. The suggestions in this book can help you take essential steps toward that freedom.

Of course, it's not enough simply to have a bold vision, to name your goals, and to identify solutions for your financial problems. There is no quick fix or overnight miracle for long-term financial instability. It is a hard walk on the Via Dolorosa while carrying all those financial burdens on your shoulders. But you don't have to carry them alone. Ask the Lord to help you bear the burden. Find your Simon of Cyrene, or let us help you with the advice we share in this book.

Getting a better handle on our financial life means being brutally honest with ourselves—about our hopes and goals, but also about where we are currently falling short. This is your chance to get honest about your current financial reality, about your beliefs about God and good stewardship, and about the habits and attitudes that you need to change in order to live a less stressful life and achieve your financial goals. While everyone's situation is unique, my husband and I have gone through similar issues and can empathize with any fears you may have. Don't give up. You can do anything God wants you to do—remember, if it's in his plan, he will show you how to get it done!

TWO

BE A GOOD STEWARD FOR LIFE

(Sam)

> Money is not the only commodity that is fun to give. We can give time, we can give our expertise, we can give our love, or simply give a smile. What does that cost? The point is, none of us can ever run out of something worthwhile to give.
>
> —**Steve Goodier**, *One Minute Can Change a Life*[2]

"Be good stewards." "Practice good stewardship." "It's Stewardship Sunday." Most churchgoing Catholics have heard these expressions over the years. But do we know what they mean and how to put them into practice in our daily lives? I'll admit that, growing up, I didn't give much thought to being a good steward. It wasn't a topic discussed at home.

And yet in hindsight, I can see that my parents practiced good stewardship, even as they raised nine of us on a middle-class salary. They made ends meet beautifully; I never felt poor or deprived. My relationship with money was gifted to me by my parents. They always taught me to adhere to that old adage, "Use it up, wear it out, make it do, or do without."

Soon after my mom had her eighth child, my dad lost his job as an airplane radio technician. This was in the early 1960s, and not many people had an abundance of money, but somehow they always found a way to help each other out.

It was around Thanksgiving time when this happened, and the church was having its yearly food drive for the needy families of our parish. As usual, my mom assembled her basket with care and delivered it to the church, and by the time she got home there was a Thanksgiving basket on our porch! Turns out our family was on the list to receive a basket. Years later, I watched my mom's eyes light up when she told me that story: "I'll never forget seeing that basket on our doorstep. It was much more generous than the one we made!" That story made a powerful impression on me. Even when we are our most generous, we can never out-give God.

Of course, my parents still struggled to make ends meet. Mom was always saying, "We had to rob Peter to pay Paul!" She had a basket of envelopes labeled for church, utilities, groceries, school clothes, and so on. She was in charge of the money, and my daddy went to work every day with one dollar in his wallet and a credit card for emergencies, one Mom made sure carried no balance. She was my first and biggest influence on how I view money to this day.

Everything we have is from God—money, possessions, talents, and time. We own nothing, even our kids; it's all on loan from God. We are entrusted with these gifts, and good steward-ship means gratefully accepting them, using them in a responsible manner, and sharing them with others. Rob and I tried to practice good stewardship as a couple even early in our dating relationship. We both felt that making our budget work in a way that would allow me to stay home with the kids was the key to laying the groundwork for our financial future.

For example, we didn't spend a lot of money on impractical gifts or fancy dates. Rob knew right away I wasn't going to expect expensive gifts or elaborate vacations when we got married. (I know, lucky guy, right?) For us, good stewardship wasn't a legalistic burden. It was more of a continuous, consistent acknowledgment that everything we have is just on loan from God, and we are to make good use of it. Once you come to this mindset, it is anything but burdensome; it is freeing and a relief. It is comforting to know that with our finances, as in all things in life, God is in charge.

This doesn't mean we didn't go out and have fun together. We dated frugally—walks to a park for a picnic lunch, swinging on the playground, or watching old movies on Rob's VCR (heard of those?). Cable wasn't a thing yet.

Of course, my extroverted personality got frustrated sometimes staying at home, watching TV. I decided to give up TV for Lent so Rob would have to take me out more. Sometimes we went to the mall to window-shop (which Rob hated), drove downtown and shared a meal, or bought some high-calorie fried food from the food court and people-watched. Once in a while Rob would splurge and surprise me with dinner at a nice restaurant. Rob's mom encouraged our budget-friendly dating by making nice dinners for us at her house for special occasions, like my homecoming dance. Rob's least favorite date was playing tennis together; he didn't appreciate my homerun hits.

These days we eat out about twice a month with gift cards that we receive as birthday or Christmas gifts. Sometimes we splurge, such as when I behave and don't get my monthly speeding ticket (I seem to be a magnet for them) or when we go out with friends. We don't feel guilty about the occasional splurges, since time with our friends is worth the extra money. These choices are *intentional, rare,* and *within our budget.*

It's important to keep dating after you're married, to help you stay connected and especially to get away from the kids. It is a small investment that keeps marriage—and faith—going strong. If you don't have extended family nearby, you may need to get creative about finding time and space for just the two of you until your children can stay home alone. Maybe you can swap sitter services with another family or organize a parents' night out at your parish with a few responsible students looking for service hours.

One of the best things we ever did, when I was pregnant with our fifth child, was to establish a 7:00 p.m. bedtime for our young kids. Once we got in the new routine, it was life changing. Our marriage grew stronger because we could spend some quality time together, instead of wearily collapsing after putting four kids under six to bed at a late hour. Our faith grew stronger because we could participate in parish programs without being concerned about the other parent having to deal with all the kids by themselves. It was easy to find a sitter or persuade relatives to babysit since most of the time the kids were sleeping before they even arrived.

The actual date doesn't need to be costly, either. One of our most memorable dates happened when we didn't have any restaurant gift cards left, but we did have a $20 gift card to a local grocery store. So, we went to the grocery store's food bar and got soup and salads. We had always wanted to try some of their prepared foods but had abstained because it was more economical to cook at home. We selected our food and sat in the little eating area where the staff usually goes for their coffee break. That $20 gift card let us sit and visit and laugh together without the kids interrupting every five minutes.

We've Only Just Begun . . . on Weddings

Knowing when to save and when to splurge is part of being life-long good stewards. As Catholics, we know there are times to fast and times to feast: the Church calendar is full of both. Have you noticed that Easter is fifty days, but all we do is complain about the forty-day fast of Lent? Christ tells us to "rejoice and be glad, for your reward will be great in heaven" (Mt 5:12). Our family life should reflect the joy of being a Catholic.

If you are just starting out as a dating, engaged, or newlywed couple, what are your financial goals? What financial worries do you have? Have you discussed these together? If necessary, go back to chapter 1 and work on setting some goals . . . together. The sooner you get your financial goals aligned with those of your beloved and start working toward them, the smoother your relationship will be. Marriage ain't always a bed of roses. Marriage is real, raw, in-the-dirt tough at times. Don't make it harder on yourselves.

Planning and paying for a wedding is the first opportunity many couples have in getting this fasting-and-feasting balance right. Comparing your lists of "essentials" will tell you a lot about each other's values and priorities. This will help set the tone for how you resolve conflicts and make decisions throughout your married life (no pressure). For better, for worse, forever.

In the days leading up to our marriage, Rob and I found ourselves playing "Let's Make a Deal" with his dad. As a wedding gift, Rob's dad offered to pay for a week-long honeymoon in the

Caribbean or give us the cash equivalent. Did we want door number one or door number two?

That was easy! We took the cash and banked it, then spent our honeymoon at a friend's house at the shore. The reason it was an easy decision for us was because we had discussed finances early in our relationship and come to a frugal mindset together. If we weren't on the same page, that decision would have been more difficult to make.

A year later, that money, along with all the cash gifts we received as wedding presents, became our seed money for opening a Christian bookstore. Without that money, we could not have opened the store and served God for ten years in it. At the time, we assumed we were practicing good stewardship by saving as much money as we could. We didn't know what turn it would take. We just knew that for us it would be better to have cash in the bank than a savage tan.

Remember that a wedding is just one, sacramental day and marriage is a lifetime. Please don't wreck your finances on an over-the-top wedding. Have a great day with good food, good friends, good music, and good fun. Just don't forget that when you get back from the honeymoon, all of life's obligations will be waiting for you. (If you'd like more details about how our family does weddings, check out the free downloadable resource "Weddings the Fatzinger Way" on the Ave Maria Press website at www.avemariapress.com/products/catholic-guide-to-spending-less-and-living-more.)

Lessons for the Seasons of Finance

Good stewardship takes on different forms during the various stages of life. Throughout our thirty-plus-year marriage, we have experienced different "seasons of finance": getting started as newlyweds, being married with young children (including health challenges and job changes), helping young adults launch their own lives, and getting older and approaching retirement. Along the way, we have made many mistakes, but we have tried to learn from them and have come out the other side stronger and wiser. While it didn't always seem so at the time, working through the mistakes strengthened our marriage.

Things will look different for each family, but certain basic lessons and principles apply to all.

Lesson 1: You're never too young (or too old) to be a good steward.

In chapter 10, we will take an in-depth look at raising financially independent children. For now, let's briefly touch on teaching kids about money. It is never too early to start talking to your kids about money. They need to know at an early age why we do or don't do things. Obviously, we have to learn these things ourselves first if we are to pass them on to future generations.

For instance, around our house you will hear the endless refrain, "Turn off the lights, shut the door, and don't take more food than you are going to eat." We aren't saying these things because we are mean or just to hear ourselves talk. We are trying to get across the point that leaving the lights on costs us money, not only in higher electricity bills but also in light bulbs burning out faster. Money that is wasted is gone forever; if we spend $100 a month more on food and utilities than we need to, that is $100 that cannot be used for more productive purposes: investing it, helping the poor, paying down debt, and so on.

Kids need to learn to be responsible in small ways so that later in life they can be trusted with larger responsibilities.

Teaching them to turn out the lights when leaving a room will
make it that much easier when they are maintaining and paying
for an entire house when they get older. We tell our kids often,
"You need to have self-control in the small things, so when you
grow up you can have self-control with the big things." When
our kids were little, we would give them a bowl of popcorn and
say, "Okay, this is saint practice, you can only eat one piece at a
time." This taught them moderation and self-control. Of course,
we don't do that all the time—just when we need the extra practice in self-control!

Kids are kids, of course—they will sometimes push back
against parental limits. So instilling discipline and accountability
when they are young is important. Recently, I found our ten-
year-old son listening to an audiobook that we had told him he
couldn't listen to until he was twelve and had read the book first.
I told him, "If we can't trust you not to be sneaky with a small
thing like this, how are we to trust you when you get older and
have lots of temptations?"

Delayed gratification can be a tough lesson to instill in children, but (like compound interest) it reaps great rewards later.
Mick Jagger probably said it best: "You can't always get what you
want!" Teaching kids to have patience and to save up for what
they want helps them tremendously when they are older, as our
daughter Lizzie says:

> If we wanted something beyond the basics, we had
> to buy it. We all got jobs early. By thirteen we were
> babysitting or walking dogs and by fifteen or sixteen
> we were working at a grocery store, concession stand,
> gym, etc. Because we had to work for what we want-
> ed, it made us think if it was worth the money or not
> and be smarter with our money.

Teaching children self-control and delayed gratification is like teaching babies to fall asleep in their crib before they learn to stand. If you wait until they are old enough to stand on their own to teach them to sleep on their own, bedtime becomes a never-ending battle. (I have failed that challenge enough times to know how important that skill is.) In the same way, if you teach your children to have self-control about spending money before they hit the teen years, you will be doing them and yourself a favor.

One of the perks of teaching kids to be careful with money is that they learn to appreciate the occasional splurge. For example, going out to eat is a pretty big deal at our house (taking a family of sixteen to a restaurant requires a second mortgage and hazmat suits for the servers). Once or twice a year, we all go out together. This year we had a big family night out on the occasion of one son's wedding rehearsal dinner. Most years, it is two 32-inch pizzas at Grotto Pizza during our beach vacation. Rob also takes out each kid individually for a birthday lunch every year—and those birthday lunches create precious memories that each child will remember for life, simply because they are so rare.

Lesson 2: You can't out-give God.

Early in our marriage, when we were barely making enough each month to cover the necessities, offering a traditional tithe (10 percent of our income) was difficult. Many times, we have trusted God with making ends meet for us—financially, spiritually, and physically. And I can't think of a time when we sacrificed money or time, and things didn't work out (maybe not the way we expected, but always for the best).

One important way to tithe your time is to spend time with God in prayer. There are 1,440 minutes in a day. How many of those minutes do you currently spend in prayer, Bible study, adoration, or daily Mass? How might you find a way to be a bit more generous with the Lord?

Sometimes God gives us unexpected opportunities to share his love with others. Rob and I sponsored a child when we were first married; when I found a photo of her recently, it was as if God was reminding me to pray for her after all these years. Then six years ago we had another opportunity to sponsor a child when Unbound, an organization that works with underprivileged kids, visited our parish. I looked through the photographs and selected one of a child that looked like my son-in-law, thinking that whenever God blessed us with a grandson, he would look just like little José. I'm certain we benefit far more from sponsoring José than he benefits from us, and we enjoy getting letters from him, especially when he calls us his godparents and says he is praying for us!

Good stewardship is a gift that gives back—though the payback might arrive years after the fact. For example, the ladies and gents at our church show their love for new mothers by providing meals three times a week after the baby is born. After our twelfth child was born by C-section, I had some medical difficulties and had to make frequent trips to the hospital; a friend set up meals for us for *three months!* Now when another family has a need, it makes me happy to pay the blessing forward. One great way to teach our children about becoming good stewards is to show them what it is to be generous—letting them hop in the car with us to deliver a meal to a new mama, an elderly neighbor, or a friend in need or to drop off food at the diocesan food bank.

Sometimes God reciprocates in unexpected ways. The Gabriel Network is a ministry near us that helps pregnant women in difficult situations with counseling, job training, supplies, and housing. We have always supported this organization in every way we could—with prayer, volunteering, and financial donations. At one point God blessed us with an unexpected "return on investment"!

After baby number twelve, I had trouble getting pregnant, then experienced a miscarriage. It was a hard time for our whole family because we were all hoping for another baby. Then one day, in April of 2012, we got a phone call from the Gabriel Network saying they had an emergency where a twelve-week-old baby might need housing. Rob and I talked and prayed as a couple (the whole process took about thirty seconds while I was on hold on the phone), and we decided we would be happy to do short-term housing. A social worker from a program called Safe Family came over to interview us and discuss the steps necessary for placement. One thing led to another, and soon we were caring for little Ray as though he were our own.

During the first month Ray came to live with us, I found out I was pregnant again. I had never been happier; then, at eighteen weeks, my water broke. Two weeks later, I delivered Steven Thomas, who had already gone to be with his heavenly Father. I was completely devastated. Yes, we had been blessed with twelve children, but I was not emotionally prepared for the idea that I might no longer be able to bear more children. Having Ray around to cuddle was a great blessing to us during this time of loss. What was supposed to be a "six-month max" placement turned into more than *five years* of caring for this precious little boy. And eventually, God stepped in with a miracle: around Ray's sixth birthday, we were told we could adopt him. Learning to say yes and to trust God in all situations is challenging, but we have discovered that the paybacks are eternal.

Lesson 3: It is essential to cultivate intentional spending habits as a family.

Intentional spending (the opposite of impulsive spending) is one of the most important, foundational principles of good steward-ship and of living generously. When we were first engaged, Rob and I discussed how we thought God wanted us to live and how to use the resources we were given to achieve this. We knew we wanted to avoid debt and manage on one income, so I could be a stay-at-home mom to any children we might have.

At the beginning of our marriage, the lack of extra money taught us that certain things were not necessary for a happy and abundant life. We didn't go out to eat much the first couple years of our marriage unless our parents took us out. Rob's dad enjoyed treating us to nice restaurants, and he only made fun of me a little for taking home the leftover bread. He liked doing it because I was so appreciative of it; I didn't take it for granted.

It's such a blessing to see our children take up this inten-tional spending lifestyle. Spending intentionally doesn't always mean spending the least amount of money possible. It means considering the options and choosing the one that gives the best value. Here are some examples of how our children have taken this concept to heart:

> Find and buy high-quality used name-brand cloth-ing, outdoor gear, and sports equipment. Then resell it for a profit when you're done or pass it on. I use thrift stores, Facebook Marketplace, shopgoodwill.

com, Craigslist, eBay, Mercari, and OfferUp. (Josh, age thirty)

Do treat yourself and buy good food at the grocery store! If you have a house full of food that you aren't interested in making, you are going to end up ordering out for dinner. So buy the steak and the ice cream you like; it is still going to be a lot cheaper than eating out. (Alex, age thirty-one)

Plan ahead on the items you know you want to spend money on. Don't buy things right away if you don't need them. I have an Amazon list; I add things to it, and often if I give it a few days, I decide I don't need it. (Lizzie, age twenty-six)

Can you think of any area of your life right now where God might be challenging you to be more intentional with the way you spend resources he has entrusted to you? In chapter 3, we will take a closer look at what it means to be an intentional spender and discuss the virtues of prudence and diligence.

Lesson 4: Mentors are valuable allies as you embrace your vocation.

When our first child was six months old, we went out on a limb and opened a Christian bookstore. After much praying and consulting with friends and family, we decided this was what God wanted us to do. As I mentioned earlier, we used our wedding money plus the money saved from my pre-wedding job to open the store.

During the first year of the bookstore, I worked during the day with the baby while Rob was at his job at the bank. Rob worked the evenings and Saturdays at the store, and I learned to manage our home. Part of learning was spending lots of time with women who mentored me. My daughter and I had meals with a wonderful big family many nights while Rob worked. Not only did they teach me hospitality but also I learned how to host and feed a large crowd. They also supported my prayer life by discussing our faith and saying a family Rosary together. It was like on-the-job training to prepare me for my future big family.

We took no money out of the store the first year; we reinvested the profits and built up the business. We lived on Rob's slowly increasing bank salary. Little did we know while negotiating leases and ordering fixtures and products that baby number two was on the way! Having two babies fourteen months apart prompted another leap of faith. Rob quit his bank job, and we lived on the $25,000 a year we were able to pay ourselves from the store's profits. While this wasn't an optimal situation for the newly married, with help from God, family, and friends, we made it through those early years with our marriage intact.

We never really felt poor because our friends and family were always around to offer emotional support. Thank God they all stood by us in our decisions, whether it was to have another baby, homeschool, open our own business, or so much more. They might not always have agreed with us, but they supported us. And God has continued to bless our efforts.

We owned that bookstore for ten years. It provided for us until Amazon.com came along. After a few years of rapidly decreasing sales, we decided to close down the store and move on to the next chapter in our journey. This was a stressful time as we wondered what we would do for work and money. Shortly after closing the bookstore, Rob took a job in the IT field, and that is what he has been doing for the last twenty years.

Taking to heart these four lessons on stewardship—honoring God with how you spend the resources he has entrusted to you—is an important step toward achieving financial freedom. Before we move into the next chapter and focus on intentional spending in greater detail, take some time to consider where God might be asking you to grow in these four key areas.

HOMEWORK

- When did you first become aware of the call to be a good steward of the things God has given to you? Have you been a good steward with your money, time, and talents? How is God asking you to pass this lesson on to other members of your family?
- Are you generous with God and others in how you use your time, possessions, and money? Do you give God the best part of your day? How has God been generous with you?
- How do you support your home parish, as well as friends and family members going through a hardship? When was the last time you accepted help? Which was harder and why?
- What does it mean to embrace your vocation? How can you be a better role model for your family, friends, and neighbors?

THREE

BECOME AN INTENTIONAL SPENDER

(Rob)

My husband and I both work less than forty hours a week. We have three kids and a good, comfortable life, and no, we don't make a lot of money. We can do this by being very intentional with our spending and spending on what's important to us. We bought a house that is less expensive than we could afford and prioritize our "fun spending." By working less than full-time and "hacking" our schedules to work different days (I do shift work, and he has his own company), we get more time with our precious little angels and save thousands of dollars every month. Work smarter, not harder!

—**Alex Fatzinger**, age thirty-one

Okay, Sam has had your undivided attention for the last two chapters. Now it's my turn! This chapter is all about spending. Who doesn't love to spend? Even Sam loses her head at a garage sale where everything is a quarter. This can be part of the problem: Sometimes we like to spend too much and lose our perspective. Thankfully, our faith and the sacrament of Confession can help us get back on track, as we receive grace to grow in wisdom and self-control.

Intentional (or "mindful") spending is spending money *consciously* after assessing your needs *prudently* and considering your options *diligently*. What does prudence have to do with it? Consider what the *Catechism of the Catholic Church* has to say: "Prudence is the virtue that disposes practical reason to discern our true good in every circumstance and to choose the right means of achieving it" (*CCC* 1806). Not everything that seems urgent turns out to be a real need. As our eight-year-old son says, "Wants are things we don't really need, like an iPod, and needs are things that are important, like food." And almost invariably, true needs can be filled in a variety of ways.

Diligence is one of our family's favorite virtues. We try to teach the kids to always work a little harder, look for opportunities at work to go the extra mile, and not sit back when there looks like nothing to do. Make sure you find something to do, clean the house before the parents get back from babysitting, don't sit and waste time watching TV or playing on your phone. Diligence is the kid who gets up early to do her schoolwork so she can get to her job later and not fall behind in school. Diligence is the college kid who doesn't miss a class, doing extra credit, or utilizing the professor's office hours and teaching assistant's aid when they are trying to get a better grade. (Mind you, because they are paying for the credits not us, time and money is on their clock and wallet). Take one example that is a big issue for many families: daycare. When both parents work the same days and hours away from home, someone else needs to take care of their kids. Many couples spend thousands of dollars a year for the best-quality childcare they can afford because this is rightly important to them. Our daughter Alex and her husband looked at their options and decided to go a different way—choosing work that allows them to switch off, so that one of them can always be home with their children. Neither of them works full-time, so the financial sacrifice is real. But for them, intentional spending is putting their resources into creating a schedule that lets them be together as much as possible, even if it means having to buy secondhand clothes, not eating out, and cutting cable.

Four Steps to Intentional Spending

Intentional spending means spending money according to your personal priorities and values, not how and when others expect you to spend it. With intentional spending, you know where your dollars and cents are going. You decide your priorities and invest in those first. You learn to plan for and deal with unexpected bills. You stop buying "gotta haves" that you forget about shortly after purchase and that just clutter up your home. You use your money in more positive ways. You tell your money where to go and what to do.

With intentional spending, you control your money—it doesn't control you! Intentional spending involves four key steps:

- Step 1: Figure out your highest priorities and goals.
- Step 2: Create a budget. List all income sources and expenses.
- Step 3: Get out of debt. Pay off your credit cards and other high-interest debt. If you can't control your spending while using credit cards, switch to using a debit card or cash-envelope system.
- Step 4: Save *and* have fun. Don't be a total Scrooge.

Okay, let's take these steps one at a time.

Step 1: Figure out your highest priorities and goals.

I have always wanted a Harley-Davidson motorcycle. I saved for one for years, and somehow that money turned into a remodeled kitchen for Sam. Love does weird things to you. Personally, I think a motorcycle is more important than new countertops and cabinets, but I seem to be in the minority. God took my big dream and turned it into something that blessed even more people—the sixteen people under my roof, to be exact.

Do not be afraid to dream big! Our God is a big God, and he wants to bless his faithful servants (see Matthew 25:14–30). When we take good care of the time, talents, and treasure he entrusts to us, he blesses us beyond our wildest dreams. You might not always get exactly what you ask for, but you won't be disappointed. His plans are best.

So, what are your financial goals? Write them down and prioritize them. Do you want to retire early? Be debt-free in a few years? Take dance lessons and become a Rockette? Finance a new chapel or library at your parish? Maybe you want to start your own business or go back to college and finish your degree. Whatever your goals are, write them down in order of importance.

If you are married, do this exercise separately and again with your spouse and see what goals you have in common. Discuss the goals you wrote down that you don't share, and come to an agreement about if, and where, they belong on the list.

As previously mentioned, our two highest priorities are to stay debt-free and for Sam to stay home with the kids. These are lofty goals, especially in today's financial climate. Let's be honest—our culture prizes instant gratification, Ivy League education financed by student loans, and bountiful credit to pay for new cars and lavishly furnished houses.

Sam and I were blessed to start our marriage with no debt other than the mortgage on the town house we bought. We furnished the town house with hand-me-downs, thrift-store finds, curb treats, and garage-sale furniture. The only thing we purchased new was a bed. (I draw the line at used mattresses.)

Sam worked outside our home until the birth of kiddo number one. We faithfully saved her paychecks so we would have money for the future and get accustomed to a one-income lifestyle. We ended up using those savings to open the bookstore, and we made a relatively seamless transition to running the store. We did things this way because it was the only way to achieve our goals, short of robbing banks or playing the lottery.

Priorities change over time. Keep your list up to date. Our current highest priority is for me to retire in the next five years—maybe switch to part-time work and then fully retire sometime after that. It would give me more time to play with our grandkids (seven and counting) and to run.

Keep in mind that your priorities may also change before you achieve them. At the time we are writing this book, the world is in the midst of the coronavirus pandemic, and our retirement accounts, like many others', now look like an all-you-can-eat-buffet after the Fatzingers show up. But we are staying the course and investing money in our retirement accounts every paycheck just as we did before the pandemic began.

Step 2: Create a budget.

Near the end of the book of Genesis, there is a story about the patriarch Joseph—the guy with the jazzy coat whose brothers sold him to slave traders en route to Egypt. In just a few short years, Joseph went from slave to second-in-command to the pharaoh himself. In chapter 41, we get a bird's eye view of the reason why budgeting is an important part of good stewardship. God sends the pharaoh a dream, which Joseph obligingly interprets for him: "Seven years of great abundance are now coming throughout the land of Egypt; but seven years of famine will rise up after them, when all the abundance will be forgotten in the land of Egypt. When the famine has exhausted the land, no trace of the abundance will be found in the land" (41:29–31).

Now, most of the time God doesn't send us dreams of shriveling wheat sheaves and skinny cows to let us know there is trouble ahead. But as we can see in this excellent biblical example of budgeting, God teaches Joseph, and us, why it is so important to budget and save. By saving the surplus instead of spending it during those seven years of plenty, Egypt was able to feed her people during the seven years of famine and prevent many from starving. That's why emergency funds are such an important part of any budget.

In part 2 of this book we will get more in-depth into budgeting, debt reduction, and saving. But for now, let's look at budgeting with a broad lens.

You are the CEO of your personal finances. You and your spouse hold all the responsibility for what happens with your money. That responsibility can seem daunting and intimidating. But if you start thinking of your household finances as your own small business that needs dispassionate overseeing, you will be well on your way to putting your financial house in order. The more you can take emotion out of the equation, the better job you will do. Be ruthless in creating and sticking to your budget, as any good CEO who wants to keep his job would be. This doesn't mean you have to track every penny until the day you meet your Maker. But you need to learn to monitor your spending and compare it against your budget, so you know what you have and where it is all going.

Step 3: Get out of debt.

If you feel like you're in over your head with credit card debt and can't relate to our story, just keep reading. Most of us at some point in our lives have to learn how to handle credit, and in many cases, that means learning from our mistakes!

I'm no exception. Between finishing college and getting engaged, a span of about one year, I acquired $1,000 in credit card debt—a decent sum in the late 1980s for a guy just out of college and working an entry-level job. That debt then snowballed, as I went out after work with friends and bought stuff that seemed important at the time. I also took out a $3,000 loan for a used car.

Then Sam's and my relationship got to the point that we wanted to spend the rest of our lives together, and we got serious about living on one income. So during our twelve-month engagement, we paid off the car loan and the credit card. It was painful at times, but it was one of our top two priorities. Since paying those debts off in early 1989, we have remained debt-free other than our mortgage.

Why has this been so important? Not everyone will agree, but we came to the conclusion that most debt is odious. Every dollar spent on finance charges is a dollar that can't be spent on something more meaningful. If you look at all the things you need to squeeze into your budget, you will realize that paying 18 percent interest or higher to buy things you can't even remember after a few months is financial suicide.

Remember, credit card companies are not your friends. As long as you make only the minimum payment each month, they are happy. But with minimum monthly payments it can take years to pay off that fancy dinner or pair of Jimmy Choos—or my multiple pairs of K-Mart blue-light specials, for that matter.

Credit card companies love it when customers make just the minimum payment each month. It is a legal form of financial bondage. They want you to keep paying only the minimum forever. Why? Here is an actual example, pulled from one of my credit card statements.

Let's say my current credit card balance is $3,826.33. At an interest rate of 16.99 percent and a minimum payment of $38 per month, it will take me *thirteen years* to pay off, at a total cost of $8,071. That's an additional $4,244.67. (Note the rate of 16.99 percent. Bear in mind that the interest rate of a typical savings account is less than .06 percent. Let that sink in for a minute.)

I am not picking on banks; I worked at one for eight years. And I'm not saying you shouldn't own a credit card: We know emergencies are a fact of life, and sometimes a credit card is the only resource we have to cover an emergency. But if we want to be the boss of our money instead of letting our finances boss us around, we must get out of that high-interest cycle. Pay off the debt and build up an emergency fund, so you aren't forced to use credit cards.

We need to exercise the virtues of *prudence* and *diligence* to practice intentional spending and get into the habit of living within our means. It will be a struggle and often not a lot of fun. It may take years in some cases, but it will be worth the battle. God does not want his people to be burdened by debt—just ask St. Matthew, who is the patron saint of finances. This applies to car loans, student loans, and personal loans. Any high-interest loan falls into this category.

Loans for new cars hold a special place of distaste for me. Why do so many people buy brand-new cars on credit? Yes, the newest Corvette looks awesome. But what is wrong with a car that is a few years old and half the cost of the brand-new version?

We have spent the last thirty-five to forty years buying well-maintained cars that are three to fifteen years old. Between Sam and me and our nine driving-age kids, we have purchased around thirty cars over that time frame. The cars have ranged in price from $500 (a fifteen-year-old Hyundai that is still running after two years of our teen abusing it) to $19,000 (a three-year-old fifteen-passenger van that is running strong after ten years and that we will probably have for another ten years).

The current average new car loan interest rates range from 5 percent (for those with a great credit rating) to 12 percent (for those with poor credit). Yes, we know there are 0 percent interest rate deals out there, for those with the best of credit scores. But there is no such thing as a free lunch. The car dealerships aren't charging 0 percent because you have a nice smile and a charming personality. They need to push certain models of their cars. And to get those special rates you normally have to forgo any cash incentives they are offering. Do you really want to make payments for up to seven years on a vehicle that starts losing value the moment you drive it off the dealer's lot? That new car smell is nice, but you can buy an air freshener for less than a dollar. Now, if you are worth millions and set for life, buy that new Corvette, and get me one.

Step 4: Save and have fun.

To paraphrase Dean Wormer from the movie *Animal House,* all saving and no spending is no way to go through life. Scrimping and saving day after day, year after year, is burdensome. If you never buy anything fun for yourself, you are likely to snap and go on a spending bender. We had to learn this the hard way. There was a time when we seldom spent money on anything that wasn't a need. And we found that being overly Scrooge-like leads to a drab life.

Eventually, we loosened up and started spending money more freely. Heck, we even get extra guacamole at Chipotle now. Our older kids think we are millionaires because we buy paper towels now, though only if they are on sale!

Create a little wiggle room in your budget so you can treat yourself on occasion. Moderation is the key. We aren't talking about weekend getaways to the Bahamas or 14-karat gold rosaries. Get your nails done, go out for a nice dinner, buy yourself a new outfit on thredUP. If you want to splurge on something more expensive, save up the money, then have at it.

Having a little mad money in your pocket is also a good idea. Give yourself an allowance. If you're married, agree as a couple about how much discretionary spending each person is going to have each month. And once you have agreed to the amount, no criticizing what each other does with the money (assuming it's legal and moral).

I have been running daily for decades; it's my escape from the craziness at home. I go through a lot of shoes, eight to ten pairs a year. I also own a thirty-five-year-old Camaro I have been restoring for eight years. Those are my hobbies and my splurge areas. Sam, God bless her, supports my obsessions for the most part.

Sam enjoys going to consignment and thrift stores and finding deals on clothes, books, and household items. She also likes the occasional pedicure and, of course, buying gifts for the grandkids. Buying gift items that are on deep discount or clearance is one of her hobbies. She has a large cabinet filled with items she can use for occasions that call for a gift. This keeps us from having to run out to the store every time one of the kids is invited to a birthday party. All she has to do is pull out the appropriate box (girl gifts, boy gifts, baby gifts, and so on) and let the child that is going to the party pick out a present. This strategy saves on extra trips to the store and allows us to avoid both impulse buying and paying full price for gift items.

A Balancing Act: Saving for the Future

At the start of this chapter we talked about the virtues of *prudence* and *diligence.* Both of these holy habits apply equally to what you spend and what you choose *not* to spend (that is, what you save)! In chapter 9, we will explore the nuts and bolts of saving in greater detail, but right now I'd like to talk a bit about the mindset of being diligent about squirreling away your nickels and dimes (and even dollars!) for a rainy day. I know a guy who only used big bills to pay for his purchases. He would take all the coins and one-dollar bills he received in change and stash them away in a jar, then another jar, and more. One day he added up all that change and discovered he had more than nine hundred dollars!

Living a balanced life and spending intentionally requires sacrifice, self-control, and some common sense. It also involves paying attention to those little whispers that come from the Holy

Spirit. Sometimes it's easier than other times to hear, but gradually and with effort (combined with lots of prayer, scripture reading, and frequenting the sacraments), you can get better at this over time.

Do you ever pray before making a big purchase? I confess I frequently forget to do so. Sam, who is known to get a little out of control at the dollar store and thrift stores, begs the Holy Spirit to give her self-control and wisdom on any purchases. Spending some time in prayer before going car shopping, for example, would be an ideal use of time. If you're really in a financial pinch, reach out to St. Jude, the patron of lost causes—, or St. Frances of Rome, the patron of automobile drivers. (St. Eligius, patron of auto mechanics, is the go-to intercessor if you blow a gasket and your emergency fund is running on fumes.)

We have also found that prayer helps us to discern how best to help others who are struggling under the weight of a particular cross. As Christians, we need to temper prudence and diligence with compassion and come alongside those who are dealing with major health issues, handicapped children, caring for elderly parents, and other hardships. We have discovered that none of us entirely avoids suffering at certain seasons of our lives, but prayer is a powerful source of strength. The people of God and our church have many ministries available to those who are in need. After our son needed surgery, I shared with our deacon's wife that our insurance didn't cover as much of the cost as we had hoped. The next day she knocked on our door with a check from the St. Vincent de Paul Society to help us pay for some of the surgery. Our emergency fund—gradually and consistently built up over time—has eased the financial burden and kept the stress levels down.

If you are just starting on your financial journey or are recovering from a financial setback, don't beat yourself up over a small or empty savings account; just start putting away something in it every paycheck. Even if it's only a few dollars. Start that lifelong habit of saving and do it regularly. Increase the amount when you can.

HOMEWORK

- In your SLAM (Spend Less, Achieve More) notebook, write a prayer that reflects your particular needs and weaknesses when it comes to saving for the future. Speak to God about where you need help the most.
- Given your current state in life, what can you do today to become a more intentional spender?
- Does your current budget reflect your current priorities? Evaluate.
- Review your credit card statements for the past few months. Did you have more wants or needs? Where might you cut back to better meet your financial goals?
- Do you have an emergency savings account and a personal allowance set aside each month? Do you and your spouse (if you have one) agree on your financial goals? If not, schedule a meeting to discuss. If you're not sure where to begin, find a mentor.
- Have you done something fun for yourself or someone you love lately? Remember to live a little.

FOUR

PRACTICE CONTENTMENT
(Sam)

> Drive your car into the absolute ground. I just got
> rid of my 2002 Oldsmobile Alero. At the time of its
> demise, it had five warning lights lit up on the dash-
> board, two electric windows that no longer went
> up, and those were the car's good points. I got my
> money's worth out of it and, as a bonus, I didn't die
> driving it.
>
> —**Caleb Fatzinger**, age twenty-eight

I am not a big fan of the word "literally." My teens *literally* use
it all the time. But we are *literally* bombarded all day long with
ads. Everywhere we turn, there are ads. On TV, on the radio, on
sides of buses, in newspapers, on billboards, popping up on the
computer and the phone, even on the back of church bulletins.

Google, Facebook, and other social media companies know
more about you than your friends and family members do.
Everything you do on their sites and apps is tracked, tabulated,
and regurgitated back to you in the form of ads sophisticatedly
designed to part you from your money. But you can beat this
plague of consumerism in your own life by prayer, fasting, and

mindful spending. And once you do, you will find it freeing. Literally.

Saving Money Is . . . Fun?

During the early years of our marriage, Rob was just starting an entry-level career in banking. His paycheck wasn't particularly large. One of the things he would do to save money was brown-bag it for lunch. (He is a rugged introvert, so this gave him a good excuse to avoid people.) We would go to the grocery store and buy the "ends and pieces" from the deli (the end slices of meat and cheese that were packaged up and sold for around one dollar per pound). Then we would go home and make forty or so sandwiches on generic white bread. Back then you could get white sandwich bread three loaves for one dollar. Mayo went on one piece of bread and mustard on the other. Then the cheese would go on the bread with the mayo and the deli meat on the bread with the mustard. Because, as I am sure you know, yellow can't touch yellow. Yes, Rob is weird. Then the sandwiches would go in plastic sandwich bags and get stacked in our chest freezer; he would take two sandwiches for lunch each day in a brown paper bag. He would bring the bag home each day and reuse it the rest of the week. Each Monday he would "splurge" and start the week over with a new lunch bag. Rob is one of those people who is content to eat the same lunch day after day, week after week, month after month, year after year. He doesn't care about special meals and almost never eats dessert or junk food, a trait I don't relate to and one I find annoying.

It became a contest to see how cheaply we could make sandwiches. We would make forty to fifty sandwiches at a time at a cost of around 25 cents each, or 50 cents a day in the late '80s. Bringing his lunch to work became a lifelong habit that has persisted for thirty-five years. Rob prefers to eat alone, and he likes that he can make himself a tasty lunch or pack leftovers for a lot less than buying a lunch would cost. So, it's a win-win strategy for him. Occasionally he does offer it up and go out to lunch with his coworkers to celebrate a birthday or retirement or other special occasion. Skipping those types of lunches just to save a few bucks would be crossing the line from frugal to miserly . . . and being a bit of a jerk.

Contentment at Work

Especially if you're just getting started at rebooting your finances, you may find that simply cutting the fat isn't enough to get by each month. You may need to find other ways to make money, through selling things you don't use or even taking on side jobs. Maybe you need to go back to school for another degree or certification to get a better job (check out our downloadable resource "College the Fatzinger Way" at the Ave Maria Press website at www.avemariapress.com/products/catholic-guide-to-spending-less-and-living-more), or maybe you need to downsize your wardrobe, house, or car. Ask God to show you what he has in mind.

Side jobs can help to achieve a specific goal. For years, during the time we owned the bookstore, Rob mowed yards part-time. He had a small trailer to haul the mowing equipment around, and he cut ten yards per week from April through September to help make ends meet. His work ethic is in his DNA, which has been passed on to our kids: Our eighteen-year-old is currently working a second job to pay his college tuition, delivering food for DoorDash. The hours are very flexible, and the pay is good ($15–$20 per hour).

Five years ago, we decided to declutter the house and sell some of our junk on eBay. It was amazing how many things we found to sell. Most of them we couldn't remember why we had bought in the first place. Rob sold a set of Franklin Mint Sterling Silver Coins of the Caribbean that he had purchased back in the late '80s. He has no idea why he bought them. It was just one of many regrettable purchases made over the years.

We discovered that people will buy almost anything on eBay. We sold nearly $6,000 worth of items that we had dug out of our closets and attic. If you don't want to deal with the hassle of selling things online, find someone with that talent or side gig. We have a wonderful friend in our town who sells books and sometimes other treasures for others for a 20 percent fee. It is worth it for us when we are busy with life to drop off a box of books at her door with our name on it and get a small check in the mail.

Can You Be Too Frugal?

If you get too carried away and obsessed with saving money, you can cross the line from frugal to miserly. The virtue of *temperance*—of not going overboard—is the key to contentment and helps us to strike a balance between frugality and miserliness. The *Catechism* reminds us:

> Temperance is the moral virtue that *moderates the attraction of pleasures* and *provides balance in the use of created goods*. It ensures the will's mastery over instincts and keeps desires within the limits of what is honorable. The temperate person directs the sensitive appetites toward what is good and maintains a healthy discretion. (*CCC* 1809, emphasis mine)

The frugal person shops at thrift stores, stocks up on ground beef when it's on sale, and buys a used car. The miser squeezes his kids' feet into shoes two sizes too small, dumpster dives behind the grocery store, and borrows his neighbor's lawnmower all summer long. See the difference?

We admit to crossing the line at times. For example, for a few weeks Rob (the self-confessed coffee addict) reused coffee grounds. Not worth it. It doesn't save that much money, and the coffee tastes like old dead skunk. So, after the experiment failed, he went back to brewing his own coffee, even when traveling. He saves plenty of money that way. Being a bit of a numbers dork, he calculated that it costs him twenty cents to make a small coffee and forty cents to make a large one. (That is using good-quality grounds, not generic.) That's much cheaper than paying two dollars or more for a coffee at a coffee shop. He claims to have been in a Starbucks fewer than ten times in his life. Of course, he could save even more money by quitting coffee and switching to tap water. But since he's been drinking coffee for forty years, the withdrawals wouldn't be pretty and might involve multiple trips to the confessional.

Spending Fasts

No, not spending money fast! Most of us don't need help doing that. We are talking about fasting from spending. Like an eating fast, but instead of no food, you get no money to spend on nonessentials. Our daughter Barbara (age twenty-five) writes: "I have started doing a 'no buy' month at least once a year, where I cannot buy anything nonessential (basically only buying food and toilet paper). This helps me slow down and avoid impulse purchases."

Years ago, we started the practice of doing spending fasts two times each year, during Lent and July, which are traditionally the time periods that work best for us. Lent is a natural time of sacrifice and fasting. And July is a quiet month for us, most days spent at the pool or beach. Pick a month when you think you will be able to stick to it. Most families will want to avoid the holiday-packed months of November and December.

The first time Rob and I discussed the idea of doing a month-long spending fast, late one June a few years ago, I thought it would be easy. Rob said, "Hey, we can do this! Let's start tomorrow."

Sure, no big deal. Boy, was I wrong.

We had a talk with all the kids about spending, or should I say *not* spending, as we would have many spending opportunities coming up in July at the neighborhood pool. We discussed not buying unnecessary items for the month, things such as swim-team shirts and snacks at the pool. One of my sons said, "This is so embarrassing. Why do we have to do this fast?"

I pointed out that it wasn't embarrassing when their father paid off our house and car notes early— or when they were able to buy their own car at age sixteen with all the money they had saved. That doesn't mean I sailed through that first spending fast without a motherly qualm. When our son's swim team took a group photo with their team shirts and he wore just a regular yellow shirt without the logo on it, I thought I would cry for him. Then and there, I swore I would not do a spending fast in the summer again while we have little kids. It was too hard. Yet every year we decide to do it again. Each of those small sacrifices taught us to be content with what we have, and I'm sure they enriched our family's spiritual life, too.

It's important not to cheat on spending fasts by stocking up ahead of time. This is an exercise in contentment, in learning to be thankful for what you have. So don't buy a bunch of stuff in the preceding month or go hog-wild the following month. There is also no online shopping and no grabbing a few nonessentials when buying groceries.

Putting these simple rules into practice can be surprisingly difficult—at least they were for us, the first time we tried it. The trickiest part was figuring out what constituted "essential": paying the mortgage, utilities, medical expenses, charitable contributions, gas, produce, and dairy, but not meat and pantry items. These fasts are a great way to clean out the pantry and freezer. That can of sardines and pearl onions will pair nicely with the bag of frozen okra and pack of chicken hot dogs you found in the back of the freezer.

"Nonessential" also means fasting from spending money in other ways, too. No eating out. No gift buying (you better be stocked up on presents). No activities that cost money. Find free things to do—hit the museums, libraries, parks, and hiking trails. Brace yourself for the temptations that will undoubtedly come to spend money on things you ordinarily would never consider buying. "Dang, I would really love to buy that Pope Francis bobblehead!" Or, "I think I need to start a gnome garden this month." It's very similar to what happens on Fridays during Lent, when you suddenly have a craving for a Double Quarter Pounder. It's the allure of the forbidden fruit. Do not give in. Resist. Pray. But if you do slip up, just start fresh the next day.

As a fun exercise, during the month of fasting, write down the things you are tempted to buy. At the end of the month, review the list. I think you will find you forgot about most of the items.

When the month is over, you should have some extra money in your budget. What should you do with it? Well, that's up to you. I would suggest using some of the money to pay down debt or bulk up your savings account. You might also tithe it to your church or your favorite charity. You could also use *some* of the money to buy an item on the list of temptations, as a reward for a successful month (assuming you still want the item in question).

Whatever you do, take a moment with your family at the end of the month to take stock and talk about what you learned from the experience, and thank God together for the gift of contentment.

Spiritual Tools to Build a Contented Life

The Church has given us some wonderful practical tools to help us grow in temperance, beat overconsumption and overspending, and be more content. Here are just a few of them.

Prayer. God wants us to talk to him and come to him with our problems. We pray for our friends, our family, the dead, and special assistance in all kinds of matters. So why not pray for guidance and strength when trying to curb overspending? Each time you reach for your purse or wallet, call on God and ask him to bless what you are doing. (It's a great deterrent to impulsive spending.)

Find a favorite scripture verse that just rolls off your tongue. Here are some examples:

- "Let your life be free from love of money but be content with what you have" (Heb 13:5).
- "Take care to guard against all greed, for though one may be rich, one's life does not consist of possessions" (Lk 12:15).
- "Do not store up for yourselves treasures on earth" (Mt 6:19).

Throughout the day, offer these verses to God. You can also offer short prayers that keep you close and connected to Jesus, such as the following:

- "Jesus, I trust in you!"
- "Lord have mercy!"
- "Come, Holy Spirit!"
- "Jesus, Mary, and Joseph, help me. Lord, thy will be done!"

Prayers like these will become your own personal cheer for strength and encouragement.

Fasting. We've discussed a spending fast, but what about a traditional fast from food? We can use this tool to help with overspending as well.

Jesus fasted for forty days and forty nights in preparation for the temptations he would face from Satan. While I don't recommend fasting for forty days straight, short fasts can be a good way to break patterns of overconsuming and overspending.

Do you want God to give you the strength to avoid going further into debt? How about skipping a meal? Or giving up dessert for a week? Maybe you have a thing for sugary coffees; could you go a few days drinking black coffee? Or, dare I say, no coffee at all? Offer a prayer with each short fast for an increase in the virtues that will help you avoid overspending.

Acts of sacrifice. Making a small sacrifice is a devotional practice most of us associate with Lent, but we can really do it any time. For instance, if you're at the store buying things you need, and you see something that is nonessential but that you would really like to have, the temptation to put it in the cart can be strong. It's not *that* much money, you think, and you could *probably* pay off the credit card bill when it comes due. Instead of acting on this reasoning, put the item back on the shelf and offer it up as a small sacrifice for someone else. Think of a family member or friend who is going through tough times and needs prayer.

These small sacrificial acts don't have to involve money. When a child is having a really hard time, I pull out the big guns: cold showers. Believe me, this is the hardest sacrifice I make, when I'm really desperate. Boy, we all better become saints for this!

Examination of conscience. Depending on your relationship with money and the state of your bank account, you may need to add spending to your evening examination of conscience. As you consider the seventh ("You shall not steal") and tenth ("You shall not covet your neighbor's goods") commandments, can you think of anything you did, and shouldn't have done? Or should have done, and didn't do? Did you . . .

- Resent, criticize, or gossip about another person out of envy or pride?
- Give generously to someone in need?
- Consume excessively or intemperately?
- Squander your resources impulsively?
- Cheat, lie, or take what does not belong to you?
- Fail to keep your promise to adhere to your budget?
- Remember to give thanks for God's blessings?

If you really struggle with spending, make sure you are getting to Confession once a month or, even better, daily Mass.

God is a miracle worker. His sacraments give us grace to be strong against temptation. I tell my kids all the time that daily Communion is my oxygen and my wisdom pill. It has guided me through years of small and large daily decisions. I believe that is what has helped me be the woman I am today. Make a special effort this week to spend time with Jesus in the tabernacle of your parish church. Ask him for the grace to be content.

HOMEWORK

- What opportunities have you had lately to practice the virtue of temperance? How have you failed or succeeded? (Include the victories. This isn't about beating yourself up.)
- How can you be more frugal without being miserly?
- Pick a time frame to try a spending fast—just a week to start is fine.
- What are you currently doing to stay close to God and to seek his help with your spending habits? How can you strengthen this area of your life through prayer, fasting, and receiving the sacraments?

FIVE

BE GENEROUS

(Sam)

Tithe to your church and/or other charities. Choose causes that you believe in and support them. Even if finances are tight, give what you can, such as with your time. It is often harder to give your time than your money.

—**Lizzie Fatzinger Rowedder**, age twenty-six

Consider this: whoever sows sparingly will also reap sparingly, and whoever sows bountifully will also reap bountifully. Each must do as already determined, without sadness and compulsion, for God loves a cheerful giver.

—**2 Corinthians 9:6–7**

One of the greatest blessings of having a comfortable level of financial stability is that it allows you to be generous with your resources. But if we are not careful, as we become more financially secure, we can become more financially selfish. So let's spend some time looking at one of the sister virtues of generosity: charity. As Christians, we can never forget that charity is to be our most defining characteristic.

In the words of Jesus himself, "Where your treasure is, there also will your heart be" (Mt 6:21). I truly believe it helped Rob and me to start our married life without a lot of extra money. We had to learn to budget from the beginning. And we quickly realized that our money was God's money, just as our marriage and family are in his hands. That meant being quick to share with those he brought across our path. And sometimes, because of the way God works, we ended up receiving more than we gave.

Take cloth diapers, for example. One of the most difficult daily tasks I had as a mom with young children was changing and washing cloth diapers for one or two kids at a time. The cloth diapers back then weren't the fancy kind that looked cute and had Velcro; I'm talking about diaper pins and rubber pants.

One advantage of using cloth diapers was that we got hand-me-downs from ecologically minded friends who started using them to help the environment and gave up after about a month. So, I frequently received fresh sets of nearly new, hardly used diapers. Back when we lived in a town house and I was expecting baby number four, I was especially grateful for those hand-me-down diapers because they helped me to pinch the pennies we needed to buy a house with a yard! We learned about generosity from having been on the receiving end so often.

When Charity Begins at Home

I love meeting new people; at church on Sunday, God help the new family! Rob has to hold me back, saying, "No new friends, we can hardly spend time with the friends we have!" I just can't help it. St. Andrew is one of my favorite saints because he was always introducing people to Christ. I love connecting people with others.

We have a friend who used to introduce us by saying, "This is Rob and Sam; they have everything but money!" We did, too. God provided everything we ever needed through his people. We learned from those who were charitable and compassionate to us and try each day to find ways to meet the needs of those God puts in our path. To use a current expression, we try to pay it forward.

Now, I enjoy being hospitable and welcoming people over anytime. But here's the thing: I am the world's worst housekeeper. I learned after my fifth child to clean the living room and worry about the rest of the house later. If the front room is clean, I can shut the doors between it and the kitchen. That way, no one can see the messy kitchen and the rest of the house beyond!

One day when I had just put baby number four down for a nap and I was pregnant with number five, I was lying on the couch for a rest. The house was messier than usual—toys all over the floor, dirty dishes in the kitchen, you name it. It was pretty embarrassing, but I needed a nap. As I lay there half-asleep, dreaming of being able to afford a maid, I heard a knock. Stumbling to the door like a drunken sailor, I found two of our local young priests standing there in their "man clothes," as my boys would say. They had just been out on a bike ride and stopped by with their lunch for a visit.

Now, I loved that they felt comfortable enough to drop in. So, I welcomed them in, kicking toys out of the way as I steered them to the dreaded kitchen. One priest waved aside my apologies; he was used to stopping by often and didn't even notice the mess. I could tell the other was embarrassed for me—no doubt *his* mom would never have let her house look like this. This embarrassed priest sat down in his white tennis shorts, then popped right up like he had sat on a tack. To my dismay, it wasn't a tack but a blob of applesauce, and it was all over his shorts! I could have hidden under the house. He just smiled and asked to go to the bathroom to clean up.

Ack! I cried in my mind. *Not the bathroom!* We had only one bathroom downstairs, and again, I am not a tidy homemaker. Who knew what it looked like?

"WAIT!" I shouted, running ahead to give the bathroom a quick wipe-down and grab any diapers hanging out in the toilet. After Father got cleaned up, we all had a good laugh, and even though that was twenty-four years ago, we still have a good laugh when we get together. Whenever he comes back for dinner (he's a glutton for punishment), we put a jar of applesauce on his seat! He says he frequently tells that story in his Sunday homilies to lighten things up and to make other mamas feel better about themselves—I took one for the team!

Loving God, Serving Neighbor

Rob says that he can attest to the fact that God opens unexpected doors for those who want to serve. Take this book, for instance. People told us for years that we should write a book, but we never thought we had anything different or important to say. But now the world is trying to find a "new normal." That new normal for many will require creative spending and budgeting as well as saving for the future. Hopefully, this book will help some people to improve their financial lives and, in doing so, their spiritual lives as well.

One of the best ways to improve your life is to learn to put others first, to live a life of service. When we choose a brave and generous path out of love for God, he always outdoes us in generosity. If we give to others, God will take care of us. Think about the generous givers in scripture, such as the poor widow of Zarephath who fed Elijah and was gifted with the bottomless oil jar (see 1 Kings 17:9–14) and the *other* poor widow in the Temple, who gave her last coin (see Mark 12:41–44). In this life and the next, God sees and remembers.

As we journey on the path to financial independence, we need to make sure we aren't becoming more selfish with our resources. We can become so absorbed with saving every dollar we possibly can that, one, we forget whose money it really is and, two, we forget to serve and love our neighbor.

During the televised Easter Mass of 2020, in the middle of the COVID-19 quarantine, our priest reminded us that we are all called to live lives of poverty, obedience, and sacrifice. Of course, depending on your current state in life, you may be called to meet those challenges differently from those around you. A single person may be called to love and serve differently than a retired person or a parent raising a family. No one will have the same game plan for their specific call to holiness.

Although the ways we serve others will vary from one person to the next, there is something we all share: We are all called to have a relationship with Christ. Again, this will look different for everyone. Some will have ample opportunity for quiet contemplation, and others (like me) have to get up very early to squeeze in some meditation time or use our chores as prayer time. While I fold laundry, I pray for the family member whose item I am folding, piece by piece, over and over again.

One of my favorite ways to pray is to take a good walk outside. Even if you are pushing a stroller, this time with God can help you connect and listen to that still, small voice. The more you connect with him—through daily prayer, going to daily Mass, or spending time in adoration—the better you will understand his will for your life. And when that happens, you can't help but love and serve those around you.

Living the Spiritual Works of Mercy

In a world filled with overly sensitive people, and where people are quick to accuse Catholics of being judgmental, it is important to provide a good witness by being unselfish and giving. We can use the spiritual works of mercy to direct our intentions and keep our motives pure. Think about which of these you've had opportunities to practice recently.

Instruct the ignorant. We are all called to teach and share the faith that was passed on to us by our parents and our parish priests.

Counsel the doubtful. I am sure we all know someone who struggles with doubt and needs a friendly ear or a teenager who is uncertain about the correct decisions to make. Sometimes the most generous way to practice this work of mercy is by listening instead of talking (my hardest task).

Admonish the sinner. Yeah, that's a tough one! Many of us find ourselves in awkward situations, wondering whether to speak up, in person or online. As the youngest of my family, many times I felt it was my obligation to tell my siblings what was right and wrong. However, I have learned that it works best when I teach by example and wait for others to ask my advice before sharing my opinion. (Unless of course they are outright bashing the Church or blaspheming God.)

Bear wrongs patiently. Wrongs can come in many different forms. Being treated harshly, falsely accused, persecuted, abandoned by a friend . . . like Jesus' Way of the Cross, perhaps? For moms, I think of bearing wrongs patiently as the continual surrendering of our own will and patiently attending to our families—never getting to eat a hot dinner, waking up over and over to attend to a sick or nursing child, and so on.

Forgive offenses willingly. What wife doesn't need to practice this hourly? Honestly, marriage is super hard! I used to nag my poor husband constantly, biting my tongue so I wouldn't say even more. I have learned now to offer it up and talk to my buddies in heaven. St. Joseph is one of my BFFs, as well as many, many others who have gone before me.

Comfort the afflicted. I am far from a compassionate person. One Mother's Day, our priest gave a beautiful homily on moms. It brought a tear to my eye until he said, "Moms are always there to cuddle you and fix your boo-boo when you fall." My kids said in a loud whisper, "Yeah, right. When we get hurt, our mom tells us to offer it up, go back outside to play, and rub some dirt on it!" I had to laugh since they are basically right!

Pray for the living and the dead. This is one that our family is actually good at. One of my favorite gifts to give someone is a Mass card. Heck, living people need Masses said, too. I also love All Souls' Day, and throughout November, I display a huge frame to which I have attached all the funeral cards I have collected from the many wakes and funerals I have attended. The kids like to remember those we love and those from church who have gone before us. We try to say the "Eternal Rest" prayer after grace, especially in November, but usually my dear husband or a teenager will say, "God bless all the dead people! Let's eat!"

Living the Corporal Works of Mercy

I am grateful that the Church has also given us the corporal works of mercy to help guide our generosity. A priest once said in his homily, "If you wouldn't take a person out for a cup of coffee, don't feel like it's your place to give them your opinion on

how they should live their life." That touched me since I sometimes feel it is my obligation to speak my mind, even when it
might not be prudent. Practicing the corporal works of mercy
has helped me to pray more and speak less, using my example to
lead others closer to Jesus. Which of these do you find yourself
practicing most often?

Feed the hungry. This can be practiced in many ways. (I do
that every day here at home.) It can be as simple as inviting
someone over for dinner, making food for your local soup kitch-
en, donating items to your town food pantry, or making a meal
for someone who just had a baby or had a loved one die. We
make food once a month for a new mom, and our diocesan
food pantry. We also try to share snacks with the people we see
standing at a streetlight with a sign.

Give water to the thirsty. This one makes me think of my
toddler, who is always thirsty, or the child who just wants to
prolong the bedtime ritual and asks for a cup of water to keep
you in eyesight as long as possible (and to lessen your stay in
purgatory).

Clothe the naked. This one makes me think of my daughter,
who last winter on a youth group trip to a large city gave her coat
to a homeless woman. But there are all kinds of ways to show
love in action. Donate the gently used clothes that we all seem
to have in such abundance. Joyfully get your kids dressed for the
tenth time in the last ten hours.

Shelter the homeless. How does your community care for
those without a place to live? We participate in a parish program
called "Warm Nights." Different churches in town take turns
hosting the homeless during the winter. The churches provide a
warm place to sleep, meals, and companionship.

Visit the sick. Again, each family must do this according to their state in life. Sometimes my kids and I go to the local nursing home for a fifteen-minute "good morning parade." We just march through the halls saying hello and smiling. Some weeks we visit a friend from church who now lives there or speak with a patient who seems low in spirits that day. (It's always a good idea to call ahead to ask if it's okay to come. Sometimes the nursing home would express a concern about the possible spread of germs, and we would skip that week.) The kids love these quick visits, and they learn a valuable lesson on how to be kind and pray for those who are sick and dying.

To this day, our kids remember a sweet lady named Fayth who asked us to take her home with us. She tried to convince me that she could fold laundry! The kids were surprised when I didn't just take her wheelchair and roll her out to our van. Trust me, I wish we could have! Some families who aren't able to make visits in person pray for the sick or send cards or color pictures for those in the nursing home. Again, whatever works best for your family's schedule, embrace that year after year.

Visit the imprisoned/ransom the captive. This act of mercy can be difficult to perform. But one thing everyone can do is pray for those who are in jail. In particular, we can pray for fellow Christians around the world who are persecuted and imprisoned for their faith. Many organizations have prison ministries that we can support with our money or time. There is also the choice of contributing to Christian relief funds.

Bury the dead. I have lived in our town for fifty-two years, I am the youngest of nine, and I have attended the same church parish since third grade. So, I am at the funeral home about three times a month, as family and friends of our community have died.

When my dad passed away, it meant a lot to me when my friends came to his wake and funeral. Ten years later I lost my mom, and the consolation I received from my friends' presence again drove home to me how important this act of mercy can be. I began to make it a priority to attend as many services as I can. We are blessed to have a beautiful cemetery at our parish, where many holy ones are buried. I have found closure and great consolation by spending time there visiting my dad, mom, sister, and the babies I have miscarried. The Church has given us a great gift in encouraging us to form a relationship with the Communion of Saints.

If we stop and think about it, many of us are carrying out the spiritual and corporal works of mercy on a daily basis with our family, friends, and the community around us. We can fine-tune these acts by doing them intentionally and by explaining their spiritual significance to our children.

Be Generous with God's Money

It is one thing to be generous with money when things are going well financially. It takes fortitude and courage to be generous when we are going through a dark time financially. And yet, this is when we are more apt to realize that all we have, money included, is from God, and it's not so much a matter of being generous as it is a matter of trusting in him. It is not more money that we require; it is more of God.

When times are tight, giving can take different forms. Your favorite charity might need someone to stuff envelopes, or the parish might welcome help in the office or with the religious education program. One month you might decide to cut back on nonessential items in order to tithe to your parish.

Again, each couple needs to make this decision together. If you are single, discuss the matter with a trusted mentor or spiritual director. It can be a struggle to make these types of decisions alone.

On the flip side, if we are doing well financially, we must not become prosperous jerks. It is a bit of a paradox, but we may tend to become *less generous* the better off we are financially. Resist the temptation to hoard your money. Do not be afraid you won't have enough if you give some away. It is not yours in the first place; it is just on loan to you to use for the Lord's purposes. Follow the example of the poor widow in the Bible who gave her last two pennies to God (see Luke 21:1–4).

The Blessings of Community

Are you afraid or embarrassed to accept help from others? I don't know if it stems from my temperament (both optimistic and practical) or if it's from growing up as the baby of the family, but I find it easy to accept the help and generosity of those around me. Of course, I reciprocate when I can, though it's not usually a 50–50 match. For example, one of my dear homeschooling buddies often planned field trips for her two daughters and would offer to take some of my older kids. If it were not for her wonderful generosity, my two oldest children never would have gone to so many special places. I was pregnant and/or nursing infants for most of their homeschooling years, so much of our fun was along the lines of walking to parks and doing arts and crafts at home.

God has placed many kind and helpful people in our lives. They are always dropping off meals, passing on hand-me-downs, or sharing carpool duties with us. I make sure the kids realize the kindness and sacrifices people make to help us. When God puts loving people like this in your life, don't be afraid or embarrassed to let them in and help you. There is nothing wrong with accepting help, especially when you really need it. It doesn't mean that you are a failure or a mooch. It just means you need help at this point in your life, and there is someone willing to help. Face it, we will all need help at times. If you can't reciprocate in the moment, just thank the Lord for providing for you—and pay it forward when you can.

Now that I am no longer pregnant and nursing all the time, I get to help and serve more often. I help at my parish and try to mentor and support young moms. I even "adopted" some little kids at our church who do not have anyone to do "Grandma things" with. In my current stage of life, I'm happy to see that the lessons we tried to pass along to our children have taken root and are bearing fruit. We love having guests over for dinner, and I always prefer that the kids bring their friends to our house rather than go out. I try to keep the freezer stocked with goodies to bring out or a pack of premade cookie dough in the fridge for quick snacks. Every Thanksgiving, our kids bring home extra guests when they come across someone who is without a family or place to go. (Our current record is fifty-five people at our Thanksgiving table.) My motto is "The more, the merrier." Rob, who cooks the Thanksgiving meal so I can socialize, probably has a different, unprintable motto.

St. Nicholas Day, December 6, is a high feast day in our house. About twenty-three years ago, someone decided to be our Secret Santa and started putting goodies on our porch for the twelve days of Christmas. We would get a knock on the door, and behold there was a bag full of goodies—three boxes of cereal on the third day of Christmas, eight chocolate bars on day eight, and so on, always with a cute poem on the side. My kids were obviously over the moon each day!

So, years later, we pick a family who's had a rough year and send them some St. Nicholas love. It might be a family who has lost a parent, experienced a miscarriage or serious illness, or lost a job. We put together a big basket of goodies and place it anonymously on their porch on the eve of St. Nicholas Day. As we deliver the goodies, it always feels like a Christmas miracle right then and there. It definitely is more blessed to give than to receive.

Nothing can take the place of being generous. It might be with your time or your talents or just offering a listening ear to someone who is lonely or in despair. I have a generous artistic friend who arranges for kids and adults to come to her home and make amazing art projects—the kind of project you could use as a gift or hang proudly on your wall. Other friends are quick to offer to take kids out for an overwhelmed mom. Making meals for new parents or the sick is part of the home contract when buying a house in our town. The people in my community would rock your world, they are that generous and kind!

HOMEWORK

- Are you afraid or embarrassed to accept help from others? If so, why?
- How can you better practice the corporal and spiritual works of mercy?
- Have you been generous with your time and money?

SIX

CHOOSE TO TRUST
(Sam)

Trust in the LORD with all your heart, on your own intelligence do not rely.

—Proverbs 3:5

Ask and it will be given to you; seek and you will find; knock and the door will be opened to you.

—Matthew 7:7

Throughout part 1 of this book, we have been looking at big ideas related to personal finances and some of the virtues that accompany them. What it all comes down to, as in all areas of life, is trusting God and seeking his guidance. Trusting God with our finances will help us get off the emotional rollercoaster that financial anxiety causes.

Once you relinquish control over your finances, you open yourself to all kinds of possibilities to serve God and others. Whatever form this takes—being open to more children, helping a relative in financial straits, or taking a leap of faith and starting a ministry—your faith and hope will grow, and you will receive abundant graces to see you through.

Tapping into Trust

Early on, when we decided to be open to children and at the same time start our own business, God didn't say, "I will guarantee a decent car, success in your business, a new job when you need it, and a massive house in your dream neighborhood." He just said, "Trust in the LORD with all your heart, on your own intelligence do not rely" (Prv 3:5).

When I gave a Theology on Tap talk to young adults about staying out of debt, I could see them cringe when I suggested they needed to "offer it up" when they felt the urge to spend mindlessly. When I say "offer it up," what comes to mind for you? Do you see your grandma, who smells like mothballs, pointing at you reproachfully? Or do you think of an opportunity to grow in the virtue of *trust*?

Maybe the phrase conjures up unpleasant memories for you. Sacrifice isn't fun; that's what Lent is for, not a book on finances, right? But in a way, it's all related. Maybe what you need right now is a kind of Lent—a chance to start over, to reevaluate, to ponder some of the choices you've made.

We can all recall wasted opportunities and experiences. So I was happy to talk to this group of young adults, some finishing college and others starting new jobs, and encourage them to establish good financial habits now. I started the evening off by acknowledging the struggles they must have in today's culture. Social media is constantly bombarding them with ideas of getting an expensive education, eating out often, buying fancy cars and 12-karat diamond engagement rings, and planning four-day wedding celebrations that would make a bridezilla blush.

Living debt-free (or simply not maxing out your credit card each month) can be nearly impossible if you don't have discipline and a strong foundation in faith. But you can do it, starting one small, sacrificial step at a time.

Little Crosses Everywhere

As Catholics, we are taught that suffering has a silver lining if we offer it up to God. Through suffering, we grow stronger in character and in our faith. Jesus says to "take up [your] cross daily and follow me" (Lk 9:23). As a mom, I do this several times each day. Each inconvenient or unpleasant situation is a small cross that I can pick up and carry as I follow along after the Lord.

What does this have to do with money? Well, a cross might be a small sacrifice, like deciding that today you are going to pack a lunch instead of spending $8.99 on that sandwich, fries, and drink at the local deli. The next day, it just might be getting up five minutes earlier to make your own coffee for only $0.23, instead of buying the $4.65 coffee at the coffee shop in town. Sacrifices like these may seem small, but they add up, and you get the bonus of growing in grace as well as saving a few bucks here and there. Doing this for a few weeks—or even a few months—won't let you save enough money to retire early, but it is a start and teaches discipline.

Hopefully, you have been setting financial goals as you work your way through this book and are creating a plan to get your savings up and your spending down, to help you achieve those goals. An occasional acronym can come in handy. Because I have a total mommy brain, I use acronyms for everything. To make my decision-making easier and to help me trust God more, I think of my name, SAM:

- S is for save, simplify, self-control, sales, slow down, and stay home.

- A is for ask for help (from God and others) and appreciate.
- M is for make a plan, minimize, make do, and make meals at home.

Good, right? So . . . what about you? What are some ways that you can save money and express your trust in the Lord's will for you and your family? To close up part 1, I'm going to look at this acronym in more depth and tell you how certain strategies have helped me to do just that.

SAMming It Up: Strategies to Help You Trust

Saving—and trusting—looks a little different for each of us. For those who are married, trusting can mean choosing to welcome a new life in difficult financial times. For others, it can be finding the courage to make a hard but necessary change at work, at home, or in the family. For the purposes of this book, trust is an act of faith, of being willing to relinquish control in order to give God room to work, as we read in the book of Proverbs: "In all your ways be mindful of him, and he will make straight your paths" (3:6).

Straight paths, right . . . who doesn't want that? What are some things we might need to let go of? Our personal desires and plans? Our physical possessions? That tall, steamy chai tea latte? Here are some ways that God helps us to walk the way of trust.

S is for simplify.

It's trendy these days to live simply. Just watch shows such as *Tiny House, Big Living* or *Tidying Up with Marie Kondo*, or listen to these words from Pope Francis in his 2014 message for World Youth Day: "Let us learn to be detached from possessiveness and from the idolatry of money and lavish spending. Let us put Jesus first."

Taking a cue from Marie Kondo, we can take the first step by decluttering our house of all the things that don't "bring us joy" (that doesn't mean teenagers) and taking care to distinguish "needs" from "wants." Our parish has a donation shed for clothes and household items. Clearing out is an ongoing battle, especially in homes with children, but it helps us in so many ways. In addition to having more room in the house, we gain the mindset that less is more. Rob recently went through all his clothes and got rid of anything he hadn't worn in the past year.

S is for self-control.

Who doesn't benefit from this great virtue? When I give up the effort to have self-mastery, everything falls apart. It may sound shallow, but when I am trying to lose weight and on one of my silly diets or fasting, I feel so much closer to God because I am sacrificing and showing *self-control*.

As of the writing of this chapter, we are mostly stuck in the house because of the coronavirus pandemic of 2020. I have been wallowing in self-pity and stuffing my face with junk food, with a house full of kids who cannot go play with their friends. When you have self-control, it is easier to make sacrifices by offering up your sufferings for others and letting go of selfish ways.

S is for sense of humor.

It does not take much effort for me to make friends with the employees in the places I regularly shop. When I was younger, with a huge pregnant belly, big van, and brood of kids walking behind me, it was clear that I had a large and growing family. The store managers and other employees would get to know me. I made sure to teach the kids to be kind, respectful, and polite, reminding them that we had to be a good example of a large Catholic homeschooling family.

In the early days of motherhood, I would pull up to our discount grocery store in my Chevy Suburban after daily Mass on Tuesdays because they had milk on sale that day. I would send in my two oldest kids, probably nine and ten, with a ten-dollar bill. One would push the cart, and the other filled it up with five gallons of milk. The entire time, the other kids and I were parked in front, watching them through the window. The clerks would get a kick out of this, and I could tell from the comments, pointing, and staring that they were explaining to customers that these two belonged to the lady out there in the car. They would sometimes gesture at me and ask if the kids could have one of the free cookies the store was famous for giving out. You could see my oldest trying to explain to the cashier that it was Lent, and they weren't allowed to have a treat that day!

My mom taught me to always become friends with the butcher, so they would let you know when they mark down the meat. One of our bigger stores usually has meat at half-price when the expiration date is within the next twenty-four hours. So I stock up the full-size freezer (an absolute must in our home) with cuts of meat that we like, usually under two dollars a pound unless it is a special treat for a birthday or date night. You should hear the comments when I am pushing the cart through the store. "Hey, lady, are you having a barbecue?" And the manager responds with, "You should see how many kids she has!"

A sense of humor also comes in handy with gift giving. I am a big believer in getting seasonal items on sale that can be used for events other than the holiday they are intended for. For example, I accidentally bumped into a huge sale at the pharmacy, 90 percent off everything from the St. Valentine's Day shelf. For under a dollar a box, I got cute valentines that had goodies in them like finger puppets and stamps. I emptied out the treats to use as gifts for my grandchildren and godchildren. I also purchased a bunch of coffee mugs with hearts and cute sayings for under two dollars, and use them as teacher gifts (I know, what teacher needs another mug?), filling them with my favorite teas or another treat.

My favorite find that day was a huge three-dollar unicorn. It didn't say anything on it about St. Valentine's Day, and my granddaughter was over the moon when she saw it in her Easter basket. Would I ever pay thirty dollars for it? Not on your life . . . but it was well worth the three dollars that I spent.

Shopping for gifts for my "gift closet" is a passion of mine. I regularly hunt through thrift stores, consignment shops, and garage sales. Twelve years ago, Rob took me to Florida for a couple-vacation to visit his dad and stepmom. We were marking my fortieth birthday and our twentieth wedding anniversary. I was exceptionally large at six months pregnant, expecting our twelfth child, and he said, "It's your birthday; I can take you anywhere you want to go." I chose the huge Goodwill superstore across the street. He almost died with embarrassment driving me there in his dad's convertible Mercedes. I was like a kid in a candy store with no kids to chase after!

S is for slow down.

Have you heard of Elizabeth Foss and her "Take Up and Read" ministry? If so, you may know the Hebrew word *selah*. It sometimes appears at the end of verses in the book of Psalms, calling for a break in the singing of the psalm. For me, it is a word that says to slow down and take a break. This, too, can be an act of surrender and trust.

In a world that is stressed out and filled with anxiety and depression, we all need to slow down. The Sabbath is God's gift to us to rejuvenate and relax. I heard somewhere, "Live Sunday right, so you can do Monday right."

This can be a challenge for extroverts such as me who enjoy running around, especially on weekends. As a stay-at-home, homeschooling mom for thirty years, I see the weekends almost like get-out-of-jail-free cards. On Friday, I start to get giddy at the thought of the baptism, birthday party, anniversary celebration, and/or birthday dinner we are invited to that weekend. Rob, on the other hand, gets a stomachache Friday afternoon at the thought of the upcoming social events and just wants to relax after a hard week of work.

It took me a while to find balance, but the past couple of years, I have learned to recognize the voice of the Holy Spirit speaking to me through my husband and to be content to stay home, especially on Sundays. We come home from Mass, eat well to celebrate Sunday since it is a feast day, and the kids play outside with each other or the neighbors. When it is nice out we love to go for a walk after dinner. If it's cold outdoors, we all lie in front of the woodstove with hot tea, reading books and watching Hallmark movies. That day of rest gets me ready for Monday when school starts early and the week of activities is on the move. As an added bonus, you save money by staying home—unless, of course, you are on Amazon's website all weekend.

A is for ask.

The gospels show a clear connection between asking and receiving the blessings of the Lord. Very often, that asking entails not just begging God for what we need from the comfort and anonymity of our prayer corner but also looking for help from within our own community. (I think it's why God created Facebook.)

A priest friend used to introduce me as the persistent widow from the New Testament (Lk 18:3–5). I took it as a compliment, as she's one of my heroes! As a Christian community, we are meant to build up one another and share and work together: "But as it is, God placed the parts, each one of them, in the body as he intended. If they were all one part, where would the body be? But as it is, there are many parts, yet one body" (1 Cor 12:18–20). This means asking for assistance when other members of the community are equipped to give it.

I realize that everyone is not comfortable with asking for help. I am so bold my husband calls me a "pit bull for Christ." So many times, I have found out that someone needed something or was in a bad way and I would have been privileged to help them if only I had known. One time, my neighbor said, "I was asked during a Bible study whom I would call in the middle of the night if I needed help, and I thought of you!" That made me jump for joy! I am so grateful that my friends feel comfortable enough to contact me if they need assistance.

Even though it can be a pain, most of the time my kids or I want something, I ask around first. Outgrown items like old skateboards, cleats, and Rollerblades are usually just junking up someone's garage, and people are relieved to give them to a neighbor who can put them to good use. Utilize sites like Freecycle and Facebook as well as family and friends. Finding things this way can be a blessing not only for you but also for the giver, too, because they get to give away stuff they do not want. I tease my friends and tell them I am giving them graces by letting them share their goodies and help me.

I know that most of you are not like me and would not ask the man in the parking lot to help you put a huge box in your car. Perhaps this could be another area of spiritual growth. It is a gift to be childlike and trusting, believing that those around you are on your team and we are here to help each other.

If you are not comfortable with asking your neighbor for help, then ask God or our friends, the saints. We have a cloud of witnesses at our beck and call 24/7, just waiting for us to turn to them. As a stay-at-home mom in the early days, with seven kids under age ten, I took full advantage of this gift, talking to the saints and asking for their intercession in all areas of my daily struggles and crosses. When my mom was not available to talk to, I would run to my mother Mary. We need to trust our heavenly Father and remember he only wants what is best for us: "Amen, I say to you, unless you turn and become like children, you will not enter the kingdom of heaven" (Mt 18:3).

I was taught that every Hail Mary was like giving Mary a rose. I felt ashamed that many of my prayers were hurried and sloppy until one day one of my mentors said to me, "Sam, if your child brings you a wildflower or a dandelion, don't you cherish it? Our Lady loves any prayer you utter!" That made me feel so much better, even when I fell asleep saying the Rosary and let my guardian angel finish for me. I have also heard that every Hail Mary of the Rosary is a blow to the head of Satan, so the more prayers, the better!

A is for appreciate.

I have often told my kids that you are not spoiled if you appreciate people and the gifts they give to you and the services they offer. I also teach them to never underestimate the power of a thank-you note. Being grateful is an important skill to teach our kids. I try to thank God each evening for the resources and people he has put on my path that day. At those seasons of my life when I was a hormonal mess, it helped me to write down three things, usually quite simple, that I was grateful for that day. It helped me to ponder the blessings of my day and go to bed on a positive note.

M is for minimize.

One of the most important ways we express our confidence and trust in the Lord is by using what we have to bless others rather than holding on to things or hoarding. This is a constant struggle for me. One bag of stuff goes out, and two more come in.

My daughter's godfather has a great rule: "My house will not gain weight." So, if something comes in, something must go out. New shoes? Get rid of an old pair. My daughter Alex has a rule that if it can be replaced for under twenty dollars, pass it on rather than keep it. When we were on a very strict budget, I tended to hold on to things. Now the rules of thumb I use are, "Would I buy this again?" and "Keep what you love." My friends are amused because my porch usually has a bag (or three) to go out weekly to our church donation shed.

M is for make do.

One of God's greatest gifts to us is creativity, which in this context means finding ways to repurpose, reuse, and recycle the things we already have. This practice is very trendy nowadays with all the recycling suggestions and DIY remakes. From a spiritual perspective, this kind of creativity reflects trust in God's providence and a desire to live simply.

Sure, your son would like a new pair of cleats, but his big brother has a practically new pair upstairs. Not to mention that worn-in cleats are more comfortable than brand-new ones. One time, my son needed new cleats, and I sent out an email to the team asking if anyone had an extra pair before I bought some. Another player's mom said they would be happy to give us a pair of hardly worn cleats that needed a good home. My son was thrilled since the cleats were way nicer than any I would have bought, and he couldn't wait to show his big brothers how cool he was.

I have been given the grace to trust our heavenly Father with all my daily problems. It doesn't mean I don't stress out or second-guess God's plans for my life and family. I don't know if it is my temperament or my birth order as the youngest (like St. Thérèse, the Little Flower), but I have a good daughterly relationship with God the Father. I know that I am fortunate and that this relationship is a growing process for many. Never give up on working on that relationship as well as utilizing the Holy Spirit, Jesus, and your guardian angel on a constant basis! These are all members of your team, committed to helping you become the saint God created you to be. Learn to breathe out, "Thy will be done," "Come, Holy Spirit," "Jesus, I trust in You," and other brief prayers that will help you get through the toughest times as well as the little daily crosses we all have to face.

HOMEWORK

- Do you trust God enough to put him in charge of your finances?
- What areas of your finances are you holding back from him?
- What would you save for if you had extra money?
- What is one way you can simplify your life today?
- How do you feel about slowing down?
- How do you make the Sabbath special?
- Do you have the courage to ask others to help you? What about your best friend, God the Father?
- Do you bear any bitterness or a grudge against your own father that might be keeping you from trusting God? If so, consider going to Confession and asking God for healing.
- What can you make do with? What can you fix? YouTube has helped us do repairs on appliances, cars, and plumbing.

PART 2

FOUR ESSENTIAL SKILLS: MAKING IT PRACTICAL
(Rob and Sam)

In part 1, we discussed some of the mindsets and virtues of the Christian life of good stewardship and how they can be applied to our finances. By now you have a better grasp on where you stand financially and the beginnings of a plan to improve your finances and trust them to God.

In this second part, we will look at four "essential skills" of good stewardship and financial freedom. These skills are foundational for debt-free living:

- Budget for life (make and stick to a budget)
- Eliminate debt (get your spending under control; spend less than you make)
- Save for what you want (this includes building up an emergency fund)
- Raise independent kids (if you have a family)

Before you can set a budget and start an emergency fund, it's important to stop the financial hemorrhage of overspending and become an intentional spender. Whether your current financial challenge was thrust upon you by an outside force (medical catastrophe, natural disaster, or unexpected job loss) or is directly attributable to your own questionable choices, the solution is the same: Regain control by managing your resources carefully according to a predetermined plan, trusting that God will give you the faith and the strength to persevere in good stewardship.

Getting out of debt is harder than *staying out* of debt. And yet, if all we have belongs to God and our spending habits are an expression of our faith and trust in him, then we can ask God to help us when we feel weak, demoralized, or defeated. When we fall down and overspend, we can ask God to forgive us and give us the strength to do better; we can also ask him to show us the root cause of this overspending and how to put things right. (If you really struggle with overspending, consider taking it to Confession, where you can receive a fresh start and the graces you need to make better choices in the future.)

As Catholics, we must do our best not to put ourselves in situations where we may give in to deadly sins such as greed, gluttony, envy, and pride. (We call that "avoiding the near occasion of sin.") For some, that may mean going into the supermarket with a shopping list and sticking to it. For others, that may mean cutting up the credit cards. Going over your credit card statements with a financial mentor or trusted friend and talking about how your actual expenses line up with your budget may also add a line of accountability that helps you meet your financial goals.

If you are married, your first accountability partner is your spouse. Sit down together after the kids are in bed and acknowledge—to each other and to God—the need to become better stewards of what God has given you. Talk about where you have messed up with your spending and what you believe God is asking you to do to manage your money better. You might begin by offering a prayer like this one:

> Thank you, Lord, for all the gifts you have entrusted to us. Thank you for all the ways you have shown your love and care for us in providing everything we need. Starting today, help us to be better stewards of what you have given us by living within our means, sharing what we have, and honoring you with our spending and saving choices. Give us the wisdom and strength to set prudent financial goals, live within our means, avoid overspending, and save for the future. Mary, Seat of Wisdom, pray for us! In the name of the Father, and the Son, and the Holy Spirit. Amen.

SEVEN

BUDGET FOR LIFE
(Rob)

If broke people are making fun of your financial plan, you're on the right track.

—**Dave Ramsey**[3]

If everyone likes you and never questions your beliefs, you're doing something wrong.

—**Fr. James Stack**

It's time to talk about everyone's favorite subject, budgeting. I realize that for some the sheer enjoyment of creating a budget ranks up there with a visit to the proctologist. I am hopeful that you won't find this chapter quite as distasteful as that.

Why have a budget? Why not just wing it? Can't we trust God to take care of it all? Won't everything work out if we don't worry about our finances and just hope in the Lord? Many people try this approach, living paycheck to paycheck and spending every dollar they make and then some. Many people are also in financial straits.

"Hoping" and "planning" are not mutually exclusive actions. While God does want to help us, he gave us the intellectual ability and the moral strength necessary to choose the good—that is, to choose virtue—and he expects us to do our part and exercise these gifts. Most people wouldn't jump out of a plane without a parachute and count on God to save them. So why do we expect God to bail us out every time we are in financial peril?

Not having a budget is like building an airplane without a blueprint. It probably won't fly. Early on when we tried winging it, our finances and marriage suffered for it. We didn't know where our money was going, and we weren't moving forward financially. We weren't sinking into debt, but we had very little in our savings or retirement accounts. We needed to make a commitment to being financially responsible and stick to it, kind of the same way we made a commitment to God.

When we first got married, we didn't have a formally written down budget. I received a paycheck twice a month, and from that, I would pay our mortgage and utility bills, make charitable contributions, and pay for gas and food. We spent whatever was left on activities and dates and put a few bucks in savings. We certainly didn't know where all the dollars were going. Life's basics were covered, but bills that were due less often (car insurance every six months, for example) were a problem. We may or may not have had enough money in our checking account to cover them, and sometimes we would have to dip into our small emergency fund. And not much money at all was finding its way into our retirement accounts, which is not surprising—who thinks much about retirement when they are twenty-something years old?

Retirement may seem far away, but it's not. Remember the man who built his house on the sand (see Matthew 7:24–27)? Building on a solid foundation is a lot of work—but you'll be glad you made the effort when the rains begin to fall.

Why Budget?

At some point in your life, you will have an epiphany: You aren't getting any younger, and it's time to get your financial house in order. In my case, this epiphany hit early—shortly after Sam and I married. I was twenty-five years old, and getting closer to thirty (which seemed "old" at the time) got me thinking about our financial future. We decided to set some concrete long- and short-term financial goals. Some of those goals were going to be easier than others to achieve. For this to work, we needed to know where our money was going. In short, we needed a budget.

Fast forward thirty years. I'm happy to report that some of our goals from the early years have been met, some are still a work in progress, and new ones have been added. At the risk of oversharing, I'll tell you about some of the goals we have met and how we are doing on our current financial goals:

- *Pay off the house early.* We paid off our 15-year mortgage in twelve years and three months.
- *Maintain an emergency fund.* We decided to save two years of bare-bones living expenses. (The coronavirus pandemic likely got you thinking about this, too.) We currently have ten months' worth saved (split 50–50 between a money market account and a CD ladder).
- *Set up a sinking fund.* Our goal was to save six months' worth of periodic expenses (nonmonthly but regular expenses such as insurance payments, annual dues, car registration, and so on) in a sinking fund (see chapter 9). We achieved this a few years ago and have now upped the goal to a year's worth of expenses.
- *Retire early.* This one is going to be tough to reach. Like many people, we took a big hit in our retirement accounts in 2020.

But we keep on saving and working toward that goal. Go big or go home.

Types of Budgets

There are dozens of budgeting methods. Let's look at three of the more popular ones.[4]

The zero-based budget

Your income matches what is going out, exactly. Income – expenses = 0. Also known as the "every dollar has a job" or the "tell every dollar where to go" budget. Whether the money is going to buy groceries or into a savings account, every dollar has a place. If at the end of the month you have $200 left, you aren't done budgeting for the month. You must decide what to do with it (pay down debt, save it, make a donation) so that the budget equals zero.

Pros and cons: People like me who are obsessed with their finances and like spreadsheets will appreciate this approach. This budget can be time-consuming, although using an app like YNAB (You Need a Budget) can cut down on the headache.

The 50/30/20 budget

Your income is split across three major categories: 50 percent goes to necessities, 30 percent to wants, and 20 percent to savings and debt repayment. If your income is $4,000 per month, you would use $2,000 on necessities, $1,200 on wants, and $800 on debt repayment and savings.

Pros and cons: Good for those who want a system that isn't too restrictive and is flexible. Less time-consuming than other methods. You can adjust the percentages as you see fit. However, you can't see as easily exactly where your money is going. This can make it harder to cut expenses out of your budget if need be.

The envelope (cash-only) system

For those who want a strict budget system but don't want to track every purchase. The idea is to get a bunch of envelopes and label them with the budget categories you want to use—food, gas, clothing, and so on. Set a spending limit for each expense category (such as $1,000 for groceries). Then, when you cash your paycheck, fill envelopes with the allotted cash, and use only that money for purchases. Once an envelope is empty, you can't spend any more money on that category for the month.

Pros and cons: This kind of budget is great for those who have trouble controlling their finances and have issues with over-spending. I have used this system in the past, but Sam did not like it at all, so we no longer use it.

I prefer to use a zero-based budget. I enjoy playing around with numbers and spreadsheets, and I do not mind spending the time required for this type of budget. I like that it shows me exactly where our money is going; this helps keep me disciplined and on track to meet our goals. If you are new to budgeting or don't like dealing with numbers, this budget might be overkill.

What budget is best? Just like an exercise program or a diet, the budget that works best is the one you will use and stick with.

How to Budget

Now let's go through the steps to set up and use a budget.

Step 1: Track all your spending for a few months.

Use a notebook or spreadsheet to record everything you spend money on each month. You might think you know where your money is going, but most people find this to be an eye-opening exercise. (I know I did.) You might discover that you spent $150 last month on toys for your cat, Mr. Buttons, or $300 on running shoes. (I've done that a time or two.)

After tracking your spending for a few months, you can create a spreadsheet. List your basic expense categories such as food, housing, utilities, gas, car maintenance, charitable contributions, medical expenses, savings, retirement, debt repayment, and so on. Then figure out how much you spent each month on average per category. You can gather some of this information from your checking account and credit card statements. Many free apps are available to track spending (see the list in the Recommended Resources section at the end of this book). I have used many methods but prefer a spreadsheet.

Step 2: Figure out your irregular or periodic expenses.

It's likely you have other expenses that you didn't need to pay during the tracking period. These periodic expenses include things such as annual dues, vacations, birthday and Christmas gifts, semiannual or quarterly insurance premiums, fees for kids' activities—anything that doesn't occur every month. Total them up and calculate what they cost you per month and add these categories to your spreadsheet from step 1.

Step 3: Tabulate all sources of income.

This includes your take-home wages (net, not gross), side gigs, investment income, and any other sources of income (again, consult your bank statements). If you have an irregular income that varies month to month, you may want to budget for a monthly "base salary"—basically, a monthly average of what you expect to earn throughout the year. In months of plenty, save the extra to be used in leaner months. Hopefully, your total monthly income is greater than your expenses. If not, it is time to start cutting expenses and/or increasing income.

Step 4: List your financial goals.

Be specific and figure out how much will be needed each month. What would you like to accomplish with this budgeting process? You will need to make categories for these items too. Maybe you want to pay off $5,000 in credit card debt in the next two years (that's $208.33 monthly), save $25,000 for a down payment on a house, or save 10 percent of your salary for retirement.

Step 5: Have a family meeting.

If you live alone, this means setting aside some time each month to look over how well you adhered to your budget and make adjustments as needed. If you are married, with or without children, set up a time to talk about your family's financial goals so everyone is both aware of and invested in the plan. (You might choose to make one of your goals a family trip or other attractive option, so everyone has skin in the game!)

Obviously, this needs to be done at an age-appropriate level—and you will likely want to hold separate meetings with your spouse to track your progress and to hold yourselves accountable. Remember, this is a work in progress—and we are to love people and use money (not the other way around).

At your first meeting, decide what type of budget you are going to use. Then review the expense-tracking worksheet you have already set up and decide how much money to allocate to each category going forward. To simplify the process, set up automatic payments from your checking account to your savings account, retirement account, credit card account, mortgage holder, and utility companies. Each month, review your expenses and revise your budget as your situation changes.

There are probably hundreds of ways to do a budget. These steps are meant as a guideline to get you started. We suggest you follow the budget for at least a year or until it becomes second nature and you are living within your means. To help you, I have created free, downloadable spreadsheets that are available on our website or at www.avemariapress.com/products/catholic-guide-to-spending-less-and-living-more. As you will see, I've included a sample budget—based on *our* household budget—to get you started.

Tips to Remember

Take it slow and easy. A budget can be daunting to set up and hard to stick with at first. Create a budget that you think will work for you and that you have the best chance of not quitting. Do not beat yourself up if you overspend on a category or make an unwise purchase. Regroup and give it a try again the following month.

Turn a deaf ear to naysayers. We have had people question our financial lifestyle. People criticize us for not going out to eat more often, using hand-me-downs, saving too much, and not spending enough in general. People may be critical of you if you visibly change the way you handle your money, especially if it affects them. They may wonder why you don't want to go out for drinks and dinner after work every day, why you choose to drive a ten-year-old Toyota Camry, or why you don't go out with the team for treats after every event. Your new lifestyle choices may be seen as invalidating theirs. Just explain that you are trying to get your financial house in order and leave it at that. Eventually, the critics often come around and realize you may be on to something when they see that your debt-free living has created a lower-stress lifestyle. (Feel free to gift them a copy of this book!)

HOMEWORK

- Schedule a budget planning meeting (with your spouse, if you have one).
- Track and make a list of all your expenses and income.
- Choose a budget type to use.
- Set up your budget.
- Use and follow the budget.
- Give budgeting an honest shot for a few months.

EIGHT

ELIMINATE DEBT
(Rob)

The rich rule over the poor, and the borrower is the slave of the lender.

—**Proverbs 22:7**

Not having any debt from things like credit card purchases, outside of a $5,000 loan for grad school, enabled me to buy a house on my own at the age of twenty-one. . . . I wasn't setting out to get the biggest mortgage payment I could, just a reasonable payment for a fixer-upper that I could pay on a single income. That low monthly payment (and only having mortgage debt) enabled my husband and me to do things later like reduce our hours at work and start our own business.

—**Alex Fatzinger**, age thirty-one

Ah, debt. Not one of my favorite four-letter words. None of us want it, and yet, as a wise man once said, "We buy things we don't need, with money we don't have, to impress people we don't like" (variously attributed to Will Rogers, Dave Ramsey, and Tyler Durden in *Fight Club*).

I avoid debt like I avoid music by Nickelback, yet out-of-control credit card debt is becoming more and more the norm. According to Experian's annual "Consumer Credit Review," the average credit card balance *per adult* in the United States was $6,194 in 2019—an increase of 3 percent from the previous year.[5]

Let's look more closely at that number. This means the average American couple has more than $12,000 in credit card debt. (And since lots of people have no credit card debt, many others must have *more* than $6,194.) What is more, only 35 percent of all cardholders pay off their cards in full each month,[6] so the debt grows heavier and heavier as the interest charges pile up. And that's just credit card debt. It does not include car loans, student loans, personal loans, payday loans, mortgages, home equity loans, or money owed to Vinnie, your local loan shark. No wonder couples are stressed and cite money issues as one of the top reasons for divorce (though paying for two separate households on the same income only makes financial problems worse for most people).

Friends, this is no way to go through life. It is time to get out of financial bondage. It is time to gain control of your financial future! Getting out of debt and becoming a saver is incredibly freeing. Having more control over your finances and being able to tell your money what to do reduces stress immensely. Notice I said, "more control," not "total control." Financial problems beyond your control will still occur, but you will be better equipped to handle them.

Caution: Debt Ahead

The devil uses debt as a tool to cloud our judgment and discourage us from making wise financial and spiritual decisions. "Well, you're already in the hole, what's another 200 bucks?" Or

"You can't possibly want another baby! You can barely pay for the ones you have." I remember these voices when I am tempted to push that "place your order" button on Amazon late at night.

The instant gratification received through internet commerce has spending implications for other areas of life, too. I see young adults who have fallen deep into credit card debt with college, travel, and car expenses who still think nothing of quick stops to fast-food restaurants and coffee shops. What's another $20 when you are already thousands of dollars in debt? Our twenty-one-year-old son Robert didn't get caught up in the idea of paying for an expensive "fun college experience." He says, "I still had fun going to community college and then transferring to the University of Maryland. While at times I wish I had been able to go there all four years, the money I saved and the credits I built up while attending community college were well worth it."

Still, our family has made many mistakes, some big and some small. Thankfully, our older kids can advise the younger ones on how to avoid making the same mistakes and give them suggestions on how to get back on track financially. Trust me, they don't want to hear about it from their parents, whom they assume were born during the Great Depression.

So, what's the big secret to getting out of debt? Well, maybe you've heard the expression, "The easiest way to lose weight is to not gain it in the first place." It's the same with financial freedom: *The easiest way to get out of debt is to not get into debt in the first place.* There are plenty of resources on how to get out of debt (we list a few at the end of this book to get you started). But how do you avoid going into debt in the first place—or stay out, once you've gotten yourself out?

Watch Your Pennies (and the Dollars Take Care of Themselves)

The title of this book includes a phrase that sums up the whole thing pretty nicely: "Spending Less and Living More." Another key phrase you'll want to remember is "intentional spending," which we discussed in part 1. When we invest our resources in the things that truly matter and that we truly need, we are like the servants in the parable of the talents (see Matthew 25:14–30), who spent the talents their master gave them wisely—and reaped a return for which he rewarded them.

So what does it mean to spend wisely? Here are some tips for living well, spending less, and staying debt-free:

- Ask the Holy Spirit to guide you to use your resources well. Ask him to nudge you when you are tempted to waste money or you are being given an opportunity to be generous with others.
- Recognize that life well lived involves discipline and self-giving. God will bless you when you tithe to your church parish and give generously to those in need. Offer God not just the leftovers but, like the widow in the Temple, the best of what you have (see Luke 21:1–4).
- Live simply and without a lot of "stuff." Sell what you don't need or use. If you haven't used something in the past year, you can likely do without it. Use Facebook Marketplace, eBay, or Craigslist, or sell things at a consignment store or a yard sale. Do what you are comfortable with. Some people are good at eBay (Rob the introvert), others at garage sales (Sam the extrovert). Find what works for you.
- Manage paperwork carefully to avoid unnecessary expenses. Track your bills to avoid late fees. Use automatic bill pay,

calendar prompts, and other schedule hacks to avoid paying unnecessary bank fees as well as late fees on bills, parking fines, and speeding tickets (I'm looking at you, Sam).

- Enjoy free things. Make a game out of who can come up with the best family fun night without spending a dime. Our library has a great collection of DVDs in addition to books. Parks and museums are often free on certain days of the week.

- Live within your means. Live in a house and drive a car you can afford. If you are spending more than half your pretax monthly income to put a roof over your family's head, it may be time to find a better situation (or additional income). Similarly, a gently used ten-year-old Toyota is not as stylish as a new Mercedes but will get you from point A to point B just as well. I mention "gently used" and "Toyota" on purpose. You want a car that has been well maintained and isn't going to nickel-and-dime you to death with repairs. And you want a car from a company that is known for quality.

- Use "found money" prayerfully and intentionally. Resist the urge to spend that next bonus or tax refund on a splurge vacation if you are trying to pay down debt or build an emergency fund. "Found money" is another way God provides— discern prayerfully what he wants you to do with it.

- Don't let unemployment derail you. If the worst happens and you lose your job, find something, anything, as soon as possible—even as you look for a better opportunity. Two of our college-age kids lost their jobs during the COVID-19 pandemic. The first kid downloaded the DoorDash app and started delivering food several times a day. After a few weeks, he got a full-time job at Safeway fulfilling internet orders. He continued to do DoorDash on the side. Kid number two called around and found a job at an ice cream shop. (Turns out ice cream is essential.)

- Advocate for yourself. Use a free credit site like Credit Karma or Credit Sesame and check your credit score. An excellent credit score (720 or higher) means lower interest rates. If your credit score is not in the excellent range, there are ways to bring it up; again, sites like Credit Karma and Credit Sesame are your friends. They have articles on how to raise your score. Call your credit card company and negotiate for a lower interest rate. When interest rates go down, check carefully to see if it makes sense to refinance your house (do not take out extra money). As opportunities arise, pray for wisdom.

- Don't fall (back) into the credit trap. Once you have done the hard work to extricate yourself, guard zealously against old habits. Track what you put on your credit card each month to ensure you can pay the bill in full. In other words, don't charge something unless you have the cash to pay it off. Avoid "buy now, pay later" and "interest-free financing" deals that merely postpone debt. The offer of "0 percent interest and six months to pay" may sound great, but companies offer deals like this because they know that the vast majority of customers who take them (around 98 percent) do not pay off the debt within six months.

Good Debt?

Let's wade into a controversial financial topic: Is all debt bad? Is there such a thing as good debt? I don't consider all debt to be bad, but I am loath to use the word *good* regarding debt. I prefer the term *intentional debt*, choosing to use debt as a tool that (like a hammer) can be managed responsibly or misused. Like Uncle

Ben in the *Spider-Man* comics used to say, "With great power comes great responsibility."

Good types of debt include low-interest loans that work to increase your income or net worth. Mortgages and business loans are examples. Bad types of debt, on the other hand, affect your finances negatively. High-interest loans, credit card balances, and car loans are examples of bad debt.

Credit card debt probably has the greatest downside, all things considered. First, studies show that people spend more when shopping with credit cards than when using cash. In addition, credit cards carry interest rates in the exorbitant 15 to 28 percent range and are generally used on purchases that add nothing to your net worth. After you have eaten the food, worn out the clothes, broken the electronics, torn up the loser Powerball ticket, and finished off the beer, all that is left is a credit card balance with a very high interest rate. This falls squarely in the bad debt category.

Now let's take a closer look at specific types of debt.

Home mortgages

Mortgages are as close to a good debt as I can think of. I am still not fond of them, and we prioritized paying off our mortgage above other financial goals. Some would suggest that keeping a mortgage is not a bad thing, considering the interest tax write-off and the lower cost of mortgages compared with other types of debt. Things were different when we had a mortgage. Interest rates were much higher. Our first house carried a mortgage at an interest rate of 10 percent. And our last mortgage was more than 6 percent. That is why we obtained a 15-year mortgage and paid extra on it each month. We also enjoy the peace of mind that comes with owning our house outright.

To better illustrate how a 15-year mortgage can save you money, here's a story for you.

Back in the day, two sisters who lived in Bethany, Mary and Martha, were both looking at new houses in Jerusalem. They wanted to live in the big city, and they each wanted a place of their own. Mary was tired of Martha nagging her to sweep the dirt floors.

After meeting a real estate agent from Century One, each settled on a place and went to see the local money lender to see how much they would have to pay monthly on their respective homes, which cost $200,000 each. Each was offered an interest rate of 3 percent and the choice of paying off the house over fifteen or thirty years. Normally the 15-year loan would have a lower interest rate, but the lender was running a Passover special.

They broke out their pocket abacus and made some quick calculations:

30-year mortgage versus 15-year mortgage
$200,000 at 3 percent
Monthly payments: $843 (30-year loan) versus $1,381 (15-year loan)
Total paid over thirty years: $303,556
Total paid over fifteen years: $248,609

Not surprisingly, Mary chose the 30-year mortgage with the much lower monthly payment. This would mean she wouldn't have to work as much and could spend more time sitting at the feet of itinerant preachers. Martha, on the other hand, liked the idea of paying $55,000 less over the course of the loan. The money saved would allow her to finally start that company she had been dreaming of to help people better organize their homes. In this case it was Martha, not Mary, who chose the better portion.

Because most of us cannot buy a house with cash, we use mortgages. (If you can afford to pay cash for a house, you probably don't need this book.) Those taking out a mortgage should make sure they have a good credit score, low debt, and some savings. Shop around for the best deal. Consider getting a 20- or 15-year mortgage if the payments fit your budget. If possible, add a little extra to your payment each month.

Car loans

Taking out a 5- to 7-year loan at 5 to 8 percent for an item that depreciates rapidly falls into the bad debt category. I understand that sometimes you have no choice but to take out a car loan; I have been there. I took out a car loan shortly after college. When my car died, I had no savings (shame on me) and an hour commute each way to work with no public transportation available. So, I bought a decent used car and took out a $3,000 loan at 10 percent interest (the glorious '80s). That car loan bugged me, and I made extra payments to get rid of it quickly. Since that time, we have never borrowed money to buy a vehicle. These loans are a poor way to use your money.

In general, we drive our cars until they are dead. We save money toward a gently used car while our current car is still functioning, to have the cash to pay for a car when the current one dies. Alas, this habit wasn't transmitted to our kids. Five of the older kids have taken out car loans. They were all in a situation similar to mine when they got out of college—old dying car and not much money. In cases like this, there isn't much of a choice if you need a car. But please buy something practical and reasonably priced.

Credit card debt

Always, always, always pay off the card in full each month. Too dogmatic? Let's take a closer look at the proper use of credit cards.

Is there a way to use credit cards properly? Many financial gurus recommend cutting up the credit cards, no matter what, and never using them. That's something to consider if you struggle with charging too much and not paying them off monthly. Some suggest reserving a credit card for emergencies and travel.

Here's what I think: It's okay to use them because of the convenience and the rewards accrued, so long as you pay them off each month. We use ours for most of our expenses, pay them off each month, and accumulate airline points. I would prefer to use them only for emergencies or convenience when traveling, but Sam is not comfortable with carrying a lot of cash and has had issues using her debit card in the past (that is, forgetting to tell the family bookkeeper about purchases and overdrawing the checking account).

If you have a low or nonexistent credit score, getting a credit card and using it properly can help build up your score. Shortly after their eighteenth birthday, all of our adult kids applied for credit cards geared toward college students. These cards have no annual fee and a credit limit of $1,000, limiting the amount of damage they can do. This allowed them to start building credit responsibly. Later, when they were buying cars and houses, having established credit made it easier for them to get loans and gave them a more favorable rate.

We have also taken advantage of the special deals offered by some stores (both online and box stores) to lure you into using their cards. For example, we have a credit card from a large online retailer named after a famous river in South America. We make a lot of purchases at said retailer. By using that particular credit card, we save 5 percent on all purchases. As with all credit cards, we just make sure to pay it off each month.

When we renovated our kitchen, we bought all our appliances from a large department store that was running a 0 percent interest special with no minimum payments for one year. We purchased the counters and cabinets from a big-box hardware store that had a similar offer. We had the cash and could have paid for everything up-front, but I preferred to put the money in a money market savings account and earn interest for the year.

Beware, this can be risky. If you use the money for other purposes during that year, and don't pay off those bills within that one-year period, you are going to be paying a year's worth of interest on the entire purchase. This strategy takes discipline and should not be used by those who struggle with staying debt-free.

Student loans

It is a sad fact that students are taking out more and more loans. The cost of college increases at a much greater rate than the inflation rate. Within our own family, while all our kids work during their college years and pay their own tuition (see the download "College the Fatzinger Way" at www.avemariapress.com/products/catholic-guide-to-spending-less-and-living-more), some of them still need to take out loans, particularly for grad school.

We have a strong aversion to student loans. That doesn't mean we are 100 percent against them, just that they should be avoided and minimized as much as possible. I asked our son Caleb to share a few useful tips on managing student debt:

> When I hit grad school I realized that, because I'm not independently wealthy, there was just no way to pay for 100–150K of graduate school during the three years I was in school. *However,* I could (and did) work part-time to pay for spending and buffer some costs.
>
> I worked four mornings a week, 5:45 a.m. to 8:45 a.m. before classes. Grad school work-study paid $15 an hour, so I took advantage of it!
>
> Keep in mind that when you take out student loans you have a six-month grace period after graduation where you don't have to make payments. Make them anyway if you can, to avoid accruing interest. Once you start paying, refinance regularly. It's a pain but use a co-signer. I was able to lower the interest rates on some of my student loans from 8 percent to 5 percent. Setting up recurring payments can usually save you 0.25 percent as well. However, with recurring payments, if you have multiple loans the bank won't allocate it toward higher-interest-rate loans, so manually go in and pay off higher-interest loans first.
>
> If you work in a public service job after graduation (government or nonprofit), take advantage of PSLF (Public Service Loan Forgiveness). Be sure to stay on top of the requirements. My wife and I use Fitbux.com (a student loan planning website). Joe, the founder, is incredible. He helps with student loan management (including refinancing, repayment plans, and will track certain payoff programs like PSLF).

At this point you might be asking yourself how spending six figures on a grad school education lines up with this book's motto of "spending less and living more." Fair enough. From an ROI (return on investment) point of view, taking out a student loan for certain professions can be a decent investment; for others, not so much. STEM, medical, business, and law degrees, as well as some of the trades—mechanic, plumber, electrician, and other skilled trades—can lead to careers right after graduation. For those careers, taking out student loans might make sense as an investment in future financial well-being. For degrees in Russian lit, art history, and women's studies, not so much.

Debt and Social Media

In the last twenty years, anxiety, depression, and stress have been on the rise, particularly among young adults, many of whom are forced to return home after graduation without the prospect of a job and whose personal debt levels are often soul-crushing. Now, I am not blaming it all on debt. Some of the stress stems from unrealistic expectations young people place on their lives as a result of what they are seeing in the media (both traditional and social). I'm talking about the constant stream of images of the so-called perfect life, full of trips, new outfits, and fancy drinks and meals. Attempts to imitate these scenes of the good life, consciously or unconsciously, tend to lead to an empty wallet, a depleted savings account, and an increasing credit card balance.

What can we do as Catholics, striving to live the call to holiness in a godless world? I say start with small sacrifices. Nothing shakes things up like a little targeted suffering. For example, what fasting does to our character can be life-altering. Whether you are fasting from food, alcohol, or screen time, you will be surprised how much you can grow.

If you want to change the world, try changing a couple of bad habits. My wife says the pandemic has thrown her off and that she is trying to get back to goal setting, spiritual growth, and mastering some annoying habits and pet sins. She's nudging me now, trying to get in a word or two about this topic. Take it away, Sam!

Let God Fill You Up *(Sam)*

When I'm feeling depleted, I find the best advice is still free: Turn off the television and spend some time meditating on the scriptures. Let the Holy Spirit speak to your heart. When we feel despair over our current circumstances or tempted to fall back into old patterns, God's Word is where we can most clearly hear his voice and grow in grace. Here is one of my very favorite passages, from Ephesians 6:

> Finally, draw your strength from the Lord and from his mighty power. Put on the armor of God so that you may be able to stand firm against the tactics of the devil. For our struggle is not with flesh and blood but with the principalities, with the powers, with the world rulers of this present darkness, with the evil spirits in the heavens. Therefore, put on the armor of God, that you may be able to resist on the evil day and, having done everything, to hold your ground.
>
> So stand fast with your loins girded in truth, clothed with righteousness as a breastplate, and your feet shod in readiness for the gospel of peace. In all circumstances, hold faith as a shield, to quench all the flaming arrows of the evil one. And take the helmet of salvation and the sword of the Spirit, which is the word of God. With all prayer and supplication, pray at every opportunity in the Spirit. To that end, be

watchful with all perseverance and supplication for
all the holy ones. (Eph 6:10–18)

Let us be good warriors, with our armor ready for battle. You
see, the battle isn't over until we are in heaven. Our family's goal
is to frequent the sacraments, including Confession, and share
our faith through example. I fail daily (heck, hourly), but with
the help of my spouse, family, friends, and community, I can
pick myself up and strive to get back on track, spiritually and
financially. And so, my friend, can you.

HOMEWORK

- Do you have debt—such as credit card debt—that you need
  to get a handle on? If so, have you prepared a plan to attack
  and eliminate it?
- Do you have a home mortgage? Is the monthly payment
  comfortable for you, or does it keep you up at night?
- Do you have a car loan you can afford? Would it make more
  sense to pay it off sooner or to sell it and get a used car? Do
  the math and decide.
- How do you feel about student loans? If you have children,
  have you discussed with your spouse how you will manage
  college expenses?

NINE

SAVE FOR WHAT YOU WANT

(Rob)

Precious treasure and oil are in the house of the wise, but the fool consumes them.

—Proverbs 21:20

Do not save what is left after spending; instead spend what is left after saving.

—Warren Buffett[7]

To parody William Shakespeare, "To save, or not to save? That is the question."

If you've waded through this book to this point, I think you know the answer to that question. Save until it hurts, then save a little more. How? First, let's tackle the bigger question of *why*. We read in the book of Proverbs, "Wealth won quickly dwindles away, but gathered little by little, it grows" (13:11).

While trusting in God and being generous toward others are hallmarks of the Christian life, we are also called to exercise the virtues of prudence, wisdom, and self-discipline. We cannot rely on others to bail us out financially or save money for us. St. Paul said, "When I was a child, I used to talk as a child, think as a child, reason as a child; when I became a man, I put aside childish things" (1 Cor 13:11). That includes expecting others to carry our burdens as well as their own. It's heartening when friends rally in times of dire emergency, but counting on others (including the government) to provide what we should provide for ourselves is neither realistic nor prudent.

We also shouldn't assume God will rescue us from our own poor choices. Faith is not a get-out-of-responsibilities card. It would be foolish to say, "I'm not worrying about saving money for retirement; I am enjoying life now. God will take care of us and provide."

Of course, God is our Father, and like any good parent he provides for us. He also lets us experience the consequences of our choices (good and bad) and gives us reason and the ability to think and act for ourselves.

Choosing not to save for retirement and expecting God to take care of it is like leaving your Porsche parked in a seedy part of town, keys in the ignition. God expects us to use the intellectual gifts he has given us (wisdom and knowledge, for example) in every aspect of our lives. We should be glad he has given us the ability to reason and figure out a plan for our future. Once set in motion, a good savings strategy not only provides for our future but relieves stress now.

Have the courage to save. It can be frightening to start a new adventure, particularly if you are not sure of the way forward. But rest assured, you are not alone, and mapping out a plan is doable for everyone.

Various holy people have said, "Courage is fear that has said its prayers." Christ emphasizes the need for prayer and fasting (see Matthew 17:21). Think of saving as fasting, and your spiritual life will soar with clarity and wisdom.

The Emergency Fund

When life happens, you need to be prepared. The car breaks down, the washing machine dies, your dentist says little Johnny needs braces, you get handed a pink slip . . . emergencies and catastrophes, big and small, pop up unexpectedly. Count on it.

Enter the emergency fund. Before we established this financial safety net, we used to scramble to figure out how to manage these curveballs. At times we were taking one step forward and two steps backward with our savings. We would drain the savings account to pay for an alternator on the car, and before we could build it back up, the refrigerator would give up the ghost.

We finally made a concerted effort and prioritized adding to the emergency fund. After struggling for years to get ahead with our emergency account savings, we now have a good cushion. When you have the money in savings, paying for a new dishwasher, for example, while not a lot of fun is less stressful.

We discussed some of the details of how we fund our emergency account early in the book—regular deposits on payday to the account, and extra money we receive from bonuses at work, side gigs, selling items on eBay, and tax refunds. The bottom line is this: We have been building up our savings for years. Some months the balance goes up and sometimes it goes down, but it is on a slow upward trajectory. Our five-year goal (which happens to coincide with our retirement goal) is to save two years of basic living expenses. In the event of another stock market crash (I'm looking at you, COVID-19), it might take a bit longer—but we are currently 40 percent of the way there.

How have we done it? Glad you asked.

Money market magic and CD ladders

Every paycheck, I put aside money for our emergency fund. I divide the money between a money market savings account at an online bank (better interest rates than a brick-and-mortar bank) and a CD (certificate of deposit) ladder I am building, also at the online bank. The CDs pay a higher rate of interest than the money market account, but in return, your money is tied up for a longer period of time. This does create extra work since you now have a money market account plus multiple CD accounts to keep track of. But online banking makes the process streamlined and painless.

There are different ways to ladder CDs. Here is the basic idea and how we do it. I have twelve one-year CDs. I spent a year funding one CD per month. So now each month I have one CD maturing. When the CD matures for the month, I add money to it and deposit it into a new one-year CD. The nice thing about the online bank we use is that there is no minimum balance required to open a CD. You can open one with whatever amount you can afford to set aside. If you are interested in the concept of CD ladders and want to learn more about the different ways to create one, Google is your friend.

The Sinking Fund

In the context of personal finances, a sinking fund is an account used for irregular expenses (not monthly) such as insurance payments and school tuition; to save for large purchases like vacations, a new roof, or a new car; or to pay large medical bills. This is an amount of money set aside regularly, separate from regular savings accounts and emergency funds.

How much do you need to put in this fund? Good question—and the best answer comes from evaluating your own spending history. We have been funding our account since 2012, and this is how we figure out the amount we need to put into it. First, we list the items we know we will have to pay in the coming year and the approximate amount each will cost:

Homeowner's insurance: $1,500
Property tax: $5,400
Neighborhood pool dues: $600
Car insurance (3 cars): $2,400
Future used car: $1,200
Car maintenance: $1,000
Medical expenses: $2,500 (We are a healthy lot!)
Tuition: $5,000
Water bill: $1,200
Total $20,800/24 paychecks = $866.66

I get paid twice a month. Each paycheck, I transfer $865 into a money market savings account named Sinking Fund. This is an approach similar to the escrow account your bank or mortgage lender creates on your behalf, adding a portion of the total cost of your property tax and homeowner's insurance to each mortgage payment and placing it in escrow to ensure that those expenses are covered each year.

Once a year, I redo the above exercise and adjust the amounts as needed. Most years I find that I have excess money in the account. If so, I will skip adding money for a paycheck or two. Some months I might not be able to put the entire amount into our sinking fund, so a few times a year I will add more to make sure we are covered.

Some of the amounts above are guesstimates. I don't know how much we will spend on car maintenance each year. In 2018 we spent $4,000 on car maintenance, mostly due to the transmission giving out on our supersized van. Most years our car maintenance costs are less than $1,000.

The medical expense estimate of $2,500 is less than the amount of our health insurance plan deductible of $3,700. Some years we spend less than $2,500. And sometimes we spend more if there is a major surgery or birth. Our potential out-of-pocket medical expenses are more than $3,700. After the deductible is met, we then have to pay 20 percent of expenses, with a total out-of-pocket potential of $6,500. Some will ask, "Why don't you use money from your HSA (health savings account) to pay the medical expenses?" The reason is for tax purposes. I provide details on HSAs in the retirement section later on in this chapter.

Saving for College

We are mean; we make our kids pay for their own college education. The download "College the Fatzinger Way," available at www.avemariapress.com/products/catholic-guide-to-spending-less-and-living-more
, has information on how they have done this and how it has worked out so far.

For those nice parents out there, saving for college in a 529 plan is the way to go.

A 529 plan is a tax-advantaged savings plan used to help pay for education. In addition to college, it can be used for K–12 education and apprenticeship programs. The two major types of 529 plans are savings plans (similar to a brokerage account, where you contribute money and invest it in mutual funds) and prepaid tuition plans (which allow you to lock in tuition at current rates).

For everything you ever wanted to know about 529 plans and then some, go to savingforcollege.com.

Saving for Retirement

Many people enjoy dreaming about retirement. Some have very noble dreams: "I'll serve the Church more when I retire," or "I'll go to daily Mass when I retire," or "I will consider the diaconate when I retire." Unfortunately, many couples never get to fulfill their dreams because one of them gets sick or dies before they can save enough to stop working.

The financial choices we make today can make all the difference. If God wants you to be his hands and feet *right now*, debt-free living allows you to share more with others. But if you envision fulfilling a different kind of mission in your later years, saving up enough to retire early will give you freedom to explore those options.

When you are in your twenties, it's tough to make saving for retirement a priority because there are so many other pressing financial concerns. You think you will have plenty of time to start saving later. When I turned thirty (back in the mid-'90s), stories of skyrocketing federal deficits filled the news, and I was worried that Social Security wouldn't be around to supplement our retirement savings. I realized we couldn't count on the government.

So I took ownership of the problem of saving for retirement. My mantra became, "Save as if Social Security doesn't exist." I decided to start saving enough money so that when we reached retirement age, we could live off our savings and investments and not have to rely on Social Security. Here we are, many decades later, and it looks like Social Security will provide us some money when we retire. But I tell my children not to count on it, and I tell them to start saving *now*. Why? As we said in the first chapter, compound interest.

How much should I save? The short answer: As much as you can. Save until it hurts, then save some more. The long answer: It depends on your current age, years to retirement, risk tolerance, current savings, pension earnings, and the lifestyle you desire in your golden years. There are many free retirement calculators online that assist in this process. I use one called FIREcalc.

Some people swear by the 4 percent rule: Save enough so that you can live on 4 percent of your retirement savings each year. In theory, the money will last until you go to meet St. Peter. A back-of-the-napkin, down-and-dirty calculation would look like this: Desired annual income in retirement x 25 = your desired savings at retirement.

So if you want to take $40,000 a year out of your retirement accounts, $40,000 x 25 = $1 million. In this case, $1 million is the savings goal.

What kind of account do I need? There are many types of investment accounts or vehicles that can be used to save for retirement. Think of these as containers that hold the money. These accounts all have different rules as to maximum contributions, maximum income limitations, if the money is taxed now or when withdrawn, and age requirements to withdraw. Some of these rules can get complex, so please do your due diligence or consult a trained financial professional.

We prioritize the funding of our retirement accounts in this order.

1. Maximize employer matching funds. Check with your human resources department to see if your employer offers matching funds to your workplace 401(k), 457(b), or 403(b) account. If so, by all means take them up on it! Let's say your

employer matches your contributions dollar-for-dollar up to 4 percent of your salary. Why leave that money on the table? If you change jobs, you can roll the money over to another fund.

2. Maximize your HSA (health savings account) savings. An HSA is like an IRA on steroids. If it were possible to be in love with a savings account, HSAs would be my sweetheart. You may be eligible for one of these through your employer if you have a high-deductible health insurance plan—or you can contribute to them privately, so long as you meet the criteria. Contribution limits are currently $3,550 for individual coverage and $7,100 for family coverage. As of this writing, those age fifty-five and older may also contribute an additional $1,000. If you don't already have an HSA, consult with a tax professional to see if you qualify.

HSAs are "triple protected" from taxes—that is, they offer three great tax breaks: (1) The contributions are tax-deductible (reducing your current taxes), (2) your HSA assets normally grow tax-free, and (3) funds can be withdrawn tax-free as long as you use them for qualified medical expenses—even years down the road. (I keep track of all medical expenses that I have paid over the years from non-HSA money. If I have $2,000 in medical expenses from 2020, I could wait ten years if I wanted to and then take $2,000 out of the account tax-free.)

3. Contribute the maximum amount allowed to your IRA (individual retirement account). In addition to HSAs, we have used two other types of IRAs: Roth and Traditional. (There are others as well, such as SIMPLE IRAs for small business employees and SEP IRAs for the self-employed. Discuss your options with your tax professional before making an investment.) If you have a spouse, be sure to max out their IRA as well—contributions are currently $6,000 maximum per person, and $7,000 if you are fifty or older (based on 2020 guidelines).

Once you have maxed out these accounts, return to your 401(k) and max that out (current contribution limits are $19,500 for those younger than fifty; $26,000 if fifty or older). If you have any money left, save it in a non-retirement brokerage account.

Should You Invest Your Retirement Account?

I should mention that I am not a professional financial planner. I have no degrees, licenses, or certificates in financial planning. I am a self-taught amateur who enjoys spending time on this, and it does take a considerable amount of time. While I'm happy to share what has worked for us, you should always consult a professional financial advisor, someone with whom you can discuss your specific needs and goals. With those caveats, here is how we invest our retirement money.

Investing money in the stock market can be frightening. The daily ups and downs can make you seasick. At one point in 2019, the value of our retirement accounts had been cut in half. This is when having the courage to keep saving through the down times shines. All during the crash, I continued to put money into all our accounts every paycheck, no matter what the stock market was doing. When the stock market was at its lowest point, I tried to look at it as getting toilet paper buy-one-get-one-free. Buying stocks on sale and rebuilding our retirement accounts seemed like the best option.

We put 25 percent in a low-cost S&P 500 Index Fund. This is basically a basket of stocks representing the largest five hundred companies in America. We invested the remaining 75 percent in the stocks of individual companies that I have researched and chosen. Is this the best way? Honestly, I am not sure. Some of my decisions have been winners and some have been stinkers, but the winners outnumber the stinkers. But I want to be the one responsible for our accounts, so I take the time to do the legwork and make the decisions. If I didn't enjoy doing this, I'd probably put all the money in an index fund and call it a day.

What do you do if you have a bumpy ride for a month or two (like when the pandemic hit)? If you are invested in index funds or if you have a financial professional handling your money, I suggest just tuning out the noise and ignoring the news as best you can. Check in every month or quarter and see how your investments are doing. I check mine daily using apps on my phone, but I enjoy this—probably too much for my own good. But for many people, closely tracking investments can be a source of real anxiety. It's okay not to feed that.

Compounding Power: The Rule of 752

> Compound interest is the eighth wonder of the world. He who understands it, earns it . . . he who doesn't . . . pays it.
>
> **—Albert Einstein**

A brief lesson on why we should all invest for retirement early and often. And why I wish I had opened a retirement account when I was just out of college. This "Rule of 752," coined by financial commentator David Bach,[8] shows how trimming even a small amount of fat from the budget can reap big rewards.

The Rule of 752 enables you to figure out how much you can save over a ten-year period by choosing to invest the money you currently spend on any weekly expense. Just multiply the amount you spend on a particular expense each week by 752 to learn how much money you would have had at the end of ten years (assuming a 7 percent return) if you had invested it instead. Let's say you spend $20 a week picking up coffee on the way to work instead of drinking the free stuff at the office. Investing that amount instead would theoretically earn you $15,040 ($20 x 752 = $15,040). Eating $25 worth of fast food for lunch every week? That equals $18,800. Drinking $30 worth of beer weekly? $22,560. Trim $100 a week from your budget by eliminating habits such as these, invest it, and you will have made $75,200 after ten years. Just another way to think of the real costs of those "harmless" little purchases we all make.

We've talked a lot about saving money. Don't forget about saving your soul, saving your family, saving your time. Find ways that work in your current state of life to enhance your faith, be truly present to your family, and find balance between work and play. You'll be glad you did.

HOMEWORK

- What emergencies have you experienced that you wished you had saved for?
- Have those emergencies motivated you to start or add to an emergency fund?
- How can a sinking fund help you in the future?
- If you have children, what is your plan to pay for college? Have you discussed this plan with your kids?
- Have you devised a plan for retirement? And started to implement it?

TEN

RAISE INDEPENDENT KIDS
(Sam)

We were not raised like most of the people I know. We were not given an allowance, and didn't have college paid for, and didn't have the latest toys and video games. It made us more financially independent and gave us a better appreciation for what we have and what we can create. It also made me a smarter consumer. When I was going to spend money on something, I'd ask myself, "What is this going to benefit?" I'd rather spend $200 on a home improvement than a coat.

—**Caleb Fatzinger**, age twenty-eight

When I was sixteen and trying to decide what I wanted to do, I thought back to what I enjoyed and did some research . . . and decided to be a financial advisor. Now that I'm twenty-three, I'm finishing my second year of being a financial advisor with my company. I wouldn't be in this career today without learning the value of money at an early age from my parents.

—**Joey Fatzinger**, age twenty-three

It was early April of 2006, everyone's favorite time of the year: tax season. As I was gathering our documents for our accountant, I realized that our oldest, who was sixteen at the time, had worked the prior year and would have to join the ranks of the rest of us lemmings and file a tax return.

In 2006 people still did taxes the old-fashioned way, with paper forms. I told our daughter we needed to do our taxes, and we would pick up the federal and state forms at our local library.

"Just give me the forms," Alex said. "I'll figure out how to do them myself." And sure enough, she did. I checked them over, and we mailed them in. That was sixteen years ago and the IRS hasn't audited her, so I guess her math was correct.

How was our sixteen-year-old able to step up like this? Was this a result of good parenting, homeschooling, being the oldest? While I would love to take the credit and claim it was all due to great parenting, the reality is a bit more complex. Temperament, natural ability, and maturity all played a part. I should also point out that not *all* our children are financial whizzes. When we asked the kids to write down their best advice to put in this book, Dom (age nineteen) wrote, "Dominic was too busy lifting weights and hanging out with his lady friends to write anything." He's one of ours. And we are proud of him, too.

It is our job as parents to prepare our children for life: handling finances, running a household, developing good work habits. To do anything less would be a disservice to them and society. Plus, you don't want them to live in your basement until they are fifty.

We have found, however, that what you can teach them—and how well they retain it—will vary from one child to the next. For that reason, raising children to achieve "financial independence" can mean different things, depending on their temperament and natural ability. For one kid, it means encouraging him to become a financial advisor. For another, it might be summoning up heroic levels of patience and kindness to help her cultivate temperance when her secondhand Jimmy Choos habit overdraws her account. And so, you need to help your kids set up goals the same way you set up goals for yourself: Figure out what's most important, create a plan, and invest resources accordingly.

Five Important Life Lessons

Just as there are core virtues related to good stewardship that we need to develop in ourselves in order to work toward financial security, there are certain mindsets we believe are important and have tried to pass along to our kids to help them live better (and not just "spend less").

Be a problem solver.

We homeschooled our eleven older kids up to the eighth grade. After that, they attended a homeschool tutorial two days a week until they met all graduation requirements (typically by the end of their junior year). The other three days of the week they worked independently on assignments from their tutors. The homeschool tutorial is a bargain compared to the Catholic high schools in our area. The tutorial is $3,000 a year per child. The local high schools are $15,000 to $25,000 a year per child.

As a board member and on-site parent/babysitter every Tuesday and Thursday at the tutorial, I like to poll graduates about what courses they found most useful after they transitioned to the next phase of their lives. To my surprise, they don't say anything about the courses in history, English, math, science, or foreign languages. What I usually hear is that the most useful course was the college/life prep elective class we offer where they learned things like how to apply for college, look for an apartment, change a tire, sew a button, set a budget, and write a résumé. You know, real-world skills.

One of the most important parts of parenting is to teach kids to solve their own problems and to get themselves out of tricky situations without your having to figure it out for them. And so, almost daily, I find myself saying, "Figure it out yourself; this is a life skill. If you truly cannot figure it out, then I will help you."

We love our kids, but we aren't always going to be around to help them and bail them out of situations. This lesson applies to basic car maintenance (like how to change a tire or check the oil), and it applies to money management. When you love someone, you need to love them in a way that helps prepare them for the future. As Proverbs 22:6 instructs, "Train the young in the way they should go; even when old, they will not swerve from it."

Appreciate what you have.

One of our parental superpowers is not spoiling our kids. This has given them an appreciation for the things they *do* have and made life easier all around.

For example, our kids love mangoes. But these tasty little fruits are normally 99 cents each, so we don't often buy them—when you are feeding sixteen, that many mangoes can blow the weekly food budget! But they are thrilled the following week when these treats go on sale for 39 cents each and Mom gets a dozen! This little exercise in self-restraint makes each bite sweeter. And that's the kind of life we want for ourselves and our kids.

That's not to say we didn't experience our fair share of spoiling as children. Rob was the oldest of three and the first grandchild, so it was natural for the adults in his family to let him have whatever he wanted. I, on the other hand, am the youngest, and had eight older siblings to dote on me. And yet, as our children have grown up and started families of their own, we have come to realize that our "no spoiling" rule has rewarded us in ways we didn't anticipate.

For one thing, learning to appreciate the little things has really helped our older kids to navigate the normal adjustments of married life. My daughter Alex offers this example:

> I have had the same car for nine years. It's an excellent car that I bought used when it was two years old. It still works well, so there has been no need to upgrade to a nicer model. We don't have the biggest or nicest house in the neighborhood, but we are content knowing that we can afford our lifestyle.

Another benefit of raising kids this way is that the occasional splurge or indulgence makes a big impression. Four years ago, the entire swarm of us descended on Arizona for our son's wedding. It was the first long-distance vacation we have ever taken as a family. And for many of our kids, it was their first plane ride.

We went out a week early to sightsee and prep for the wedding. The kids were full of wonder and amazement at all the beautiful places we visited and the adventures we had together. If they had been raised taking fancy trips, they wouldn't have appreciated that family vacation nearly so much—including the pool and hot tub at our Airbnb rental. The lemon tree in the backyard was the icing on the cake.

One of my favorite scripture passages about contentment—the ability to be satisfied with what you have—comes from St. Paul's letter to Timothy:

Indeed, religion with contentment is a great gain. For we brought nothing into the world, just as we shall not be able to take anything out of it. If we have food and clothing, we shall be content with that. Those who want to be rich are falling into temptation and into a trap and into many foolish and harmful desires, which plunge them into ruin and destruction. For the love of money is the root of all evils, and some people in their desire for it have strayed from the faith and have pierced themselves with many pains. (1 Tm 6:6–10)

Prioritize family time.

Rob and I aren't always on the same page on every topic, but when it comes to how our family spends its time, we usually agree. Since our first child was born, we have tried to lead a simple life, not running around every minute of the day, not signing the kids up for every club and sport. This principle has not always been easy to live by. At times we did not let some of our more athletic kids play on an advanced or travel sports team, mainly because we didn't have the money or time to get them to the multiple practices and expensive tournaments.

That's not to say each person can't have individual hobbies or activities—Rob's running mania is a good example. But every opportunity must pass a standard test: "What is best for the entire family?" When I was pregnant and/or nursing, I didn't want babies and kids to be stuck in the car all day while I ferried their siblings to practices and games. With a big family, it's important that each member learn to put family welfare before personal preferences.

You may feel differently about how much time your family spends in various sports activities—and there is nothing wrong with that. Some families give high priority to sports because of their children's particular skills and abilities (not to mention scholarship potential). I sometimes find myself envious of my friends who manage to balance both family life and various commitments to sports. Some couples make sports work for their family by coaching or getting multiple kids on the same team. Others seem to spend their lives running kids all over creation to make it to the next practice. We choose to make family time a priority; doing sports and activities full bore would never work for us. We would be worn too thin, and family life would suffer.

We also try to balance how we spend the Sabbath day. I dream of having a huge Sunday dinner with all my family here and grandchildren playing, but so far that hasn't worked very well. My older kids have their own schedules and lives to lead. So, we will continue to take one season at a time trying to do what is best for our whole family, not just one member.

No slacking.

Because we never had much money for extras, overindulging our kids with gifts wasn't an issue. But spoiling isn't just about buying things. It can also be letting children get away with things, staying up late, not doing their chores, using bad language, and other behavioral issues.

Catholic clinical psychologist and radio personality Dr. Ray Guarendi says it best: "I can give you the tools to teach your kids to obey, but I can't give you the energy to follow through." When I was a young mom, my kids couldn't get away with anything. But after three decades of diligence, this old mama has lost her steam, and the younger kids get away with much more than their older siblings. I beg God daily for balance and wisdom on how to raise them. The nice thing is the older kids can mentor the younger ones and teach them from example. Many times, a big kid will say to one of the younger kids who is sassing me, "Don't talk to my mom like that!"

One of the ways we build character in our children is to teach them to work hard. There are lots of chores in a large household like ours, and doing chores since they were young has instilled in each of our kids a good work ethic. Because of that mindset, all of our children have loved getting jobs and getting paid to do things that are usually easier than their chores at home. "Babysit your one kid? Sure. It is quieter there than at my home, and I can get my homework done while she's napping!" Not to mention babysitting pays ten to fifteen dollars an hour these days. Besides providing them with cash for nonessentials such as cell phones and fancy sneakers, work keeps them occupied during those slothful and temptation-filled teen years.

Take responsibility in the small things.

Fifteen years ago, we had an HGTV crew come to our home to interview us for a chance to be on their show and have one room renovated. The men were looking around upstairs and asked me why the ceiling fans in four of the bedrooms only had one or two bulbs working. I explained that my little darlings never turn off the lights, so I purposely keep dead bulbs in some of the sockets to save money. Leaving lights on in an empty room is a sure way to get on my naughty list.

Another easy way to push my buttons is to leave a door to the outside open. Every time I see an open door, I have flashbacks of my parents yelling, "Were you raised in a barn?" To this day, I am obsessed with shutting doors and turning out lights that aren't needed. Even at friends' houses. And we have nine boys who all seem to have some mental block that prevents them from closing doors and turning off lights. But eventually, the kids figure it out—usually after they have moved out and begin paying the electric bill themselves.

Another area of responsibility we emphasize is not wasting food. It's a big no-no in our family. There weren't lots of leftovers in my childhood home, but if something was on the verge of spoiling, my mom would make something out of it quickly. I try to follow her example. When we have overripe bananas or other fruit, it's time for a smoothie. If milk is going bad, the kids know it's time for Mom to make a huge batch of waffles. Veggies getting soft? Time for soup. The kids know that if I throw something out, it has to look like a science experiment gone bad.

Most of our older kids have worked at concession stands and fast-food joints. They come home from work scandalized at the amount of food people waste. (I knew I was a great mom the day my nineteen-year-old daughter Barbara asked me, "Mom, is it McDonald's or Burger King that sells the Big Mac?") This has also helped our kids realize how expensive and unhealthy a fast-food routine can become; self control is a bit easier when you see how much money it saves you! We are proud, not embarrassed, when our kids bring home untouched food that would have otherwise gone to waste. (Organizations such as Food Rescue US do a great job of fighting both food waste and hunger by matching restaurants with local community kitchens and food pantries.)

Of course, my kids sometimes take the "don't waste" principle to extremes. Shortly after we moved into a new neighborhood, I stopped by a neighbor's house to pick up my four-year-old from a birthday party and was met at the door by the dad, an old high school friend. He handed me a large bag of snack-size M&M's and said that after the piñata had been broken, my Barbara tried her best to fend off other partygoers to "collect extra candy for my brothers and sisters." After that, when the kids had finished eating pizza (the kind some strange man in a red shirt delivered to the door), Barbara asked the host if she could bring all the crusts home, "because my little brothers love the crusts!"

I will admit that, like all children, ours have needed a bit of schooling in social niceties to avoid these embarrassing moments. When our little gluttons-in-training pile their plates high with Chick-fil-A nuggets as hungry people line up patiently behind them at a social gathering, we take them aside and gently remind them that this is not their last meal. They need to just take enough and be thoughtful of others—or they can make a sacrifice and only take a small amount, until everyone has a chance to have some. I noticed a positive example of this recently at a pool party when I ran into an eleven-year-old boy who said his mom taught him not to take the last thing off a platter, in case someone else wants it.

As Rob and I have watched our kids grow up and start families of their own, we have seen how these five little life lessons have set them up for the kind of success that cannot be measured in dollars and cents. *Be a problem solver. Appreciate what you have. Prioritize family time. No slacking. Take responsibility in the small things.*

These principles have instilled in them the character they will draw on to make the sacrifices and choices necessary to achieve the financial goals they set for themselves. And for this, we needed to teach them another, equally important set of values and skills. Let's call these lessons Money Matters 101.

Money Matters 101

Especially as they reach an age when they are old enough to work outside the home for their own money, don't put off teaching your kids to be smart spenders and careful consumers. Show them how to balance a checkbook (a lost art). This will teach them discipline in handling their finances. And it also prevents overdraft fees and will help with budgeting.

Teach them to protect their financial and personal data. (Never give anyone your Social Security number unless absolutely required. Guard your account information and passwords like you would the *Mona Lisa*.) As natural teaching moments emerge, fight the urge to run in and handle things for them. Instead, slow down and explain how loans work: mortgages, car loans, and student loans. While you're at it, explain how taxes work: income taxes, property taxes, and Social Security taxes.

In addition to these practical financial tutorials, continue to bring them back to the *why* of financial responsibility. At the end of the day, everything we have belongs to God, who entrusts these resources to us so that we may do good and serve others. Here are some of the most important lessons parents can pass along to their children about life's financial realities.

Learn from your mistakes.

Don't be afraid to let your kids learn from their mistakes or to let them know that you haven't been perfect with handling your money, either. Tell them about the time you bought a pet rock and thought it was the most incredible thing ever . . . for a few days, until you realized you paid $5.99 for a rock.

Discuss their past purchases, good and bad: the quality bike they purchased at a garage sale that they have maintained so carefully— and the expensive game they just threw out that they "had to have" or that new skateboard they left out in the rain. Experiencing firsthand the letdown of a hastily made purchase as well as the exhilaration of finally getting something long desired is an important rite of passage for most kids. Learning to have self-control in the small things leads to having self-control with the big things when they grow up.

You're never too young to save.

Start teaching your kids to save at a young age. Begin with the basics: There is a limited amount of money, they can never spend more than they have, and it's important not to spend it all. They need to save some and share some.

We don't do allowances, but that doesn't mean you can't. Many families use allowances as a way to teach children how to work for money and what to do with the money they make. When they are old enough to understand the different coins, offer them a dollar for doing a certain chore, then pay them with ten shiny dimes. Explain that each time we earn a dollar, we need to save a dime (10 percent), share a dime (10 percent), and then spend the rest. Most kids will think that is very fair.

Help them pick out or create a piggy bank (you can always decorate a can or mason jar) to start the saving process. Those shiny dimes will add up fast! Once their bank starts filling up, take them to a brick-and-mortar bank and open a savings account. Teach them about interest. (We have used many forms of three saving/spend/give jars over the years.)

As a family, talk about ways to pool resources to share with the Church and with others. Encourage your children to give of their money and time. Have your kids give some of their own money to your parish church. Christmas and Lent are good times to do this. Or have them choose a special ministry or charity to help.

As I said, it's important to introduce the idea of saving and sharing while children are still very young. It will help them tremendously when they are older, and they need those lessons in self-control to get them through the teen years.

Be careful with your credit.

We now have nine kids with driver's licenses. All of them have bought their own first cars, usually before they turned sixteen, without a car loan in the bunch. Each of them worked and saved and searched for a reliable set of wheels that would get them where they needed to go. And seeing is believing: The sight of our driveway and street lined with cars is all the motivation the younger ones need to start their own car fund (our poor neighbors!).

Early and often, we have cautioned our kids about getting caught up in credit card debt. As parents, we need to be careful to model a good example here. Don't let them think that whipping out a card is all you have to do to buy things. Make sure they know not to use credit cards unless they have the money to pay them off in full each month. They need to know that they will have to pay interest (a lot of interest) if they carry a balance. Teach them that it's better to use cash or debit cards for purchases— and to exercise extreme caution when making purchases online.

Learn how to shop.

Teach your kids how to be smart shoppers and careful consumers. I know shopping with kids can be more painful than watching a Miley Cyrus music video, but take them with you and show them how to comparison shop and how to stick to a list of items drawn up ahead of time. Have them hand the money to the cashier, not a credit card, and make sure they get the correct change. If you want to improve your own grocery shopping skills, check out the downloadable resource "Feeding Your Family without Going Broke" at the Ave Maria Press website at www.avemariapress. com/products/catholic-guide-to-spending-less-and-living-more.

The lessons continue at home after the groceries are put away. Teach your kids how to turn basic ingredients into delicious meals to share with family and friends. Show them that you don't have to spend a lot of money to have a warm and inviting home, the kind of home that reflects love and hospitality. This, too, is an important part of living well and of being a good steward of the resources God has given us. If we do our jobs well, the blessings of this lifestyle will be a family legacy for generations to come.

HOMEWORK

- As a couple, decide what financial traits you want for your family or what ones you need to revisit.
- Which of the five important life lessons covered in this chapter do you think you need to work on right now with your family? Are there other lessons that you think are also important?
- What are a couple of the "Money Matters" that are particularly relevant to your family right now?
- Why is hospitality such an integral part of good stewardship and of living well? What is one way you can practice hospitality this week?

CONCLUSION
(Rob and Sam)

If you made it this far, God bless you, and thank you for journeying with us through the world of personal finances as we see it from the perspective of our Catholic faith.

We want to encourage you to continue to work with your family to develop these essential habits, mindsets, and practices. We recognize that your particular situation may be very different from ours. And yet, we believe God wanted us to share the financial vision he has given us in order to help other families overcome whatever challenges they may be facing as they seek to do his will. As St. Paul says in his second letter to the Corinthians:

> Blessed be the God and Father of our Lord Jesus Christ, the Father of compassion and God of all encouragement, who encourages us in our every affliction, so that we may be able to encourage those who are in any affliction with the encouragement with which we ourselves are encouraged by God. (2 Cor 1:3–4)

We have learned so much in writing this book. We set out to help others improve their finances, and hopefully we have. But we are the ones that learned during this process. It has given us a chance to review and tweak our own financial strategies. As we wrote this book over several months during the pandemic frenzy, there was much to contemplate and plenty of time to do it. The events of 2020 drove home the point that we have to be in top shape financially, physically, and spiritually. You never know what life is going to throw at you.

So we hope that this book provides an avenue for you to get your financial house in order, whether that means a bit of remodeling or a complete overhaul. Go over your vision and goals again. Make sure they are prioritized and start tackling them.

If there is one thing we want you to take away from this book above all, it's that it takes *discipline*, not just motivation, to get one's finances in order. And because Rob likes to use running analogies and stories, he wanted to close this book by offering the best running (and financial) advice he knows: "You will never always be motivated." Here's what Rob says:

> I run every day. Not bragging or showing off, just telling it like it is. I started running in the spring of 1978 (yes, running shoes had been invented). It was love at first run. Since it's my "thing," I decided fifteen years ago that I would run every day unless seriously injured—heart transplant, coma, and stroke are about the only acceptable reasons to take a day off from running.
>
> Things like blazing heat, ice storms, flu, injuries, and just being plain old tired can and will demotivate you quickly. Knowing that I wouldn't always be motivated to run, I made it part of my daily routine or discipline. Just like showering, brushing my teeth, and eating, running always happens, no excuses. This requires discipline and passion, not motivation. I've woken up many cold winter mornings in the dark and had to drag myself out of a warm bed and lace up the shoes and hit the streets. Motivation was not

the reason I ran on those inhospitable mornings; discipline was. When the chips are down, motivation goes out the window.

This applies to many areas of life, not just running. Finances, practicing the faith, showing up for work daily, and doing the chores around the house all take discipline. Who is motivated to go to work every morning? All the financial strategies and tips in the world won't help you if you don't have the discipline and prudence to ask God to help you implement them.

For Christians, this discipline is (or should be) an expression of our faith. It is this fundamental faith in God, and a deep-rooted desire to please him and pick up our crosses in everything we do, that has been at the heart of all the choices we have made as a family—financial and otherwise. Without a desire to live out the financial virtues in a systematic, disciplined way, all the tips, hacks, and tricks are just ideas rattling around in your brain and getting on your nerves.

Our parenting must have made some impression—or Sam has learned to bilocate—because the kids say they can hear her voice when they try to spend unwisely or waste money: "Are you really going through the drive-through again?" "Don't waste that food; you can have it for leftovers tomorrow." "Don't forget to tithe 10 percent of your money to church or a charity that means something special to you." However, we can't force them, or anyone, to change their attitude or lifestyle. If you are in debt, or just not in the financial situation you want to be in, it is up to you to be honest with yourself, make some changes, sacrifice, and start taking your spending seriously.

We have offered suggestions to help you. Pray about your situation and ask for wisdom on how you can be a better steward.

If you don't have debt but want to do more with your money to serve God's people, then look for places you can cut back to achieve that goal. Thank you for being willing to use your finances to be the hands and feet of our Savior. Many in our world need help, so narrow it down to something that speaks to your heart. God will direct you if you ask.

Finances cause problems for couples, families, and single people. We believe that stressing over finances is one of Satan's tools to trap us and make us think that it is our money, not God's. And so, we'd like to close this book with a prayer that you can offer each day—on your own or as a family—to help you find your way. We have adapted a famous prayer by Bl. Charles de Foucauld, the Prayer of Abandonment.

A Prayer of Trust and Surrender

Father, we place ourselves in your hands.
Do with us, and with all we have, what you will.
For whatever you give us, we thank you.
For whatever you allow, we trust you.
We are ready for it all. We accept it all.
Only let your will be done in us.
Into your hands we commit our lives,
All that we have and all that we are.
We offer ourselves to you to grant us great wisdom and self-control.
For we love you, Lord. And we trust you above all.
And so, we surrender ourselves, our finances, and our future into your hands without reserve and with endless confidence.
Protect and sustain us, O Lord. By your Spirit, alert us to temptation, and give us humility to turn to you for our every need. Make us grateful for all you have provided, and make us quick to share, slow to spend,

and wise in saving for the future. We ask all these things in the name of the Father, and the Son, and the Holy Spirit. Amen.

You can do this. You are capable of so much more than you know. Figure out your goals, go for big ones along with the small ones, and do them. One step at a time is how all journeys begin. Now get out there and start yours.

HOMEWORK

- What is one idea from this book that you want to apply to your life?
- What are some issues currently facing your family that you most need to surrender to God?
- When was the last time you went to Confession as a family? Consider receiving this sacrament together to strengthen your resolve to renew your family's financial situation. God will give you what you need, if you are willing to respond with obedience, trust, and faith.

ACKNOWLEDGMENTS

First, we want to say thank you to our parents. You gave us life and sacrificed daily in raising us. You were the first who taught us how to save and spend wisely. We cannot begin to list all that you have done for us over the years. We are sure you shook your heads and wondered about some of our decisions over the years, but you were always there for us and always willing to lend a helping hand. In loving memory to Barbara, Frank, and Walter. We miss you and think of you every day.

Thank you to our children. You have all been a blessing to us and turned out darn well . . . so far. (Don't let it go to your head.) We could not have asked for better children. Daily you make us laugh and cry, feel proud and exasperated.

To our grandkids and future grandkids: We and your parents love you so much. Whoever said, "If I knew how much fun grandchildren were, I would have had them first," was right on the money. You are perfect and can do no wrong in our eyes. We will always be there for you, especially when your parents are mean to you. Pop and Grammy will love you forever, like you for always.

To all our friends, especially those at Sacred Heart Parish: You have been mentors, friends, brothers- and sisters-in-arms, prayer warriors, and people we could commiserate with. You are the ones we would call in the middle of the night when broken down on a highway. We have shared many meals, drinks, laughs, runs, and Masses with you. Many of you have given your time, talents, hand-me-downs, and financial help to us in different ways over the years. You continue to inspire us and challenge us to be better Christians.

Thank you to Heidi Saxton, our first-ever editor at Ave Maria Press, for her vision, encouragement, and answers to the thousands of questions we had. To Justin McClain, who cheered us on and crossed our I's and dotted our T's when we had no clue what we were getting ourselves into. Thank you, Tom Grady, Karey Circosta, Kristen Bonelli, Susana Kelly, Stephanie Sibal, Catherine Owers, and everyone else who had patience with us learning the ropes at Ave.

I (Rob) would like to thank my bride of thirty-two years. My journey would have been a lot less interesting and probably shorter if we hadn't met. Through all the years, you have always had my back. You have loved me despite my many faults. I have been a lousy husband, questionable father, and bad Catholic over the years, yet you have always stood beside me. You put up with being a "running widow" and support, or at least tolerate, my running adventures. You are the love of my life and you are (that over-used expression) my soul mate. You are the Lucy to my Ricky, the rose to my thorn, the oil to my vinegar.

I (Sam) would like to thank God for being my best friend and giving me the life of my dreams with a great husband and many babies, and my dream home in my favorite town ever. Rob, thanks for being open to life and even taking in others who needed us, our bonus babies. You put up with my crazy personality, my constant talking, and my endless suggestions of things to do (like this book)—the world's most extroverted person marries the world's biggest introvert will be our next book. To my kids—you know you are all my pride and joy; you know it wasn't always fun being the mean parent and nagging you all to death constantly! My life will be complete when we are all in heaven together as the saints God created us to be. To my parents in heaven, who were my first teachers of trust and frugality. Thanks for taking the leap in faith to adopt a baby girl when you were already raising eight other children. To my siblings, who made me want lots of babies to enjoy the fruits of a large family. To Helen and Fatz, who were there to catch us if we fell. To Geama, Rob's mom, my best friend ever. Thank you for always helping me and being a mom to me; I don't know what I would do without you. To all my soul sisters who pray and put up with my daily text messages. You all are my sounding boards and mentors dragging me kicking and screaming to Christ. To all the priests and religious orders who have helped shape my faith and have helped me in my many apostolates over the years. Thanks for saying yes!

Last, but far from least, we thank God for all he has done for us. He brought us together over thirty-five years ago, at a keg party, of all places. He has been with us every step of the way, probably shaking his head frequently at the things we have done. He hasn't always said yes, but he has always guided us in the right direction when we were smart enough to listen. Thy will be done!

+JMJ+

NOTES

1. Mike and Alicia Hernon, "Unity," January 31, 2020, *Messy Family Minutes,* https://www.messyfamilyproject.org/mfm-12-unity.

2. Steve Goodier, *One Minute Can Change a Life* (Life Support System Publishing, 2009).

3. Dave Ramsey, "If Broke People Make Fun Of Your Financial Plan Then You're Right On Track," November 19, 2019, *The Dave Ramsey Show Live,* https://www.youtube.com/watch?v=stJFk1df4vk.

4. "Five Different Types of Budgeting Methods," SoFi, January 21, 2020, https://www.sofi.com/learn/content/types-of-budgeting-methods.

5. Matt Tatham, "2019 Consumer Credit Review," Experian, January 13, 2020, https://www.experian.com/blogs/ask-experian/consumer-credit-review.

6. Ethan Wolff-Mann "The Average American Is in Credit Card Debt, No Matter the Economy," February 9, 2016, https://money.com/average-american-credit-card-debt.

7. Alice Schroeder, *The Snowball: Warren Buffett and the Business of Life (*New York: Bantam Books, 2008).

8. Noel Whittaker, "The Latte Factor and the Rule of 752," *Sydney Morning Herald,* November 15, 2018, https://www.smh.com.au/money/planning-and-budgeting/the-latte-factor-and-the-rule-of-752-20181115-p50g5y.html.

RECOMMENDED RESOURCES

The following apps, websites, and books have helped us over the years.

Budgeting and Money-Tracking Tools

EveryDollar—everydollar.com

Easy Budget—easybudgetblog.com

Goodbudget—goodbudget.com

Mint—mint.com

Personal Capital—personalcapital.com

PocketGuard—pocketguard.com

YNAB (You Need a Budget)—youneedabudget.com

Credit Score and Credit Cards

Credit Karma—creditkarma.com

Credit Sesame—creditsesame.com

NerdWallet—nerdwallet.com

All-Around Financial Guidance

Chris Hogan—chrishogan360.com

Dave Ramsey—daveramsey.com

Dough Roller—doughroller.net

Fatzinger Family—FatzFam.com

Early Retirement

Mad Fientist—madfientist.com
Mr. Money Mustache—www.mrmoneymustache.com

Books

How to Manage Your Money: An In-Depth Bible Study on Personal Finances, by Larry Burkett
The 7 Habits of Highly Effective People, by Stephen R. Covey
The Complete Tightwad Gazette: Promoting Thrift as a Viable Alternative Lifestyle, by Amy Dacyczyn
The Millionaire Next Door: The Surprising Secrets of America's Wealthy, by Thomas J. Stanley and William D. Danko
Your Money or Your Life: 9 Steps to Transforming Your Relationship with Money and Achieving Financial Independence, by Joe Dominguez and Vicki Robin
Everyday Millionaires: How Ordinary People Built Extraordinary Wealth—and How You Can Too, by Chris Hogan

Online Selling

Craigslist
eBay
Facebook Marketplace
Mercari

INDEX

Sam and Rob Fatzinger are the parents of fourteen and the grandparents of seven whose financial success story has been featured in publications including *The Washington Post*, Marketplace.org, *EpicPew*, *Patheos*, *Aleteia*, *The Oakland Press*, and the *Daily Mail*, as well as on *The Chris Hogan Podcast* (Dave Ramsey Ministries), *Girlfriends*, and *EWTN Pro-Life Weekly*.

Sam is a homemaker and homeschooler who serves as a principal of St. Peter the Rock Homeschool Tutorial and as a parish, family, retreat, and homeschool coordinator. Rob is a software quality assurance manager at ManTech International.

The couple lives in Bowie, Maryland.

Babystepsjmj.blogspot.com
fatzfam.com
sardoniccatholicdad.blogspot.com
Facebook: Sam Lancaster Fatzinger
Twitter: @FatzFam
Instagram: @samjmj
Pinterest: Sam Lancaster Fatzinger

Gary Zimak is the author of *Let Go of Anger and Stress!* and *Give Up Worry for Lent!*

www.followingthetruth.com
Facebook: Gary.Zimak.speaker.author
Twitter: @gary_zimak

AVE

Ave Maria Press

Founded in 1865, Ave Maria Press,
a ministry of the Congregation of
Holy Cross, is a Catholic publishing
company that serves the spiritual and
formative needs of the Church and its
schools, institutions, and ministers;
Christian individuals and families; and
others seeking spiritual nourishment.

———

For a complete listing of titles from

Ave Maria Press

Sorin Books

Forest of Peace

Christian Classics

visit avemariapress.com